T0051719

Selling
from Your
Comfort
Zone

Selling
from Your
Comfort
Zone

The Power of
Alignment Marketing

STACEY HALL

BK®
Berrett–Koehler Publishers, Inc.

Copyright © 2022 by Stacey Hall

All rights reserved. No part of this publication may be reproduced, distributed, or transmitted in any form or by any means, including photocopying, recording, or other electronic or mechanical methods, without the prior written permission of the publisher, except in the case of brief quotations embodied in critical reviews and certain other noncommercial uses permitted by copyright law. For permission requests, write to the publisher, addressed "Attention: Permissions Coordinator," at the address below.

Berrett-Koehler Publishers, Inc.
1333 Broadway, Suite 1000
Oakland, CA 94612-1921
Tel: (510) 817-2277
Fax: (510) 817-2278
www.bkconnection.com

ORDERING INFORMATION
Quantity sales. Special discounts are available on quantity purchases by corporations, associations, and others. For details, contact the "Special Sales Department" at the Berrett-Koehler address above.
Individual sales. Berrett-Koehler publications are available through most bookstores. They can also be ordered directly from Berrett-Koehler: Tel: (800) 929-2929; Fax: (802) 864-7626; www.bkconnection.com.
Orders for college textbook / course adoption use. Please contact Berrett-Koehler: Tel: (800) 929-2929; Fax: (802) 864-7626.
Distributed to the U.S. trade and internationally by Penguin Random House Publisher Services.

Berrett-Koehler and the BK logo are registered trademarks of Berrett-Koehler Publishers, Inc.

Printed in the United States of America

Berrett-Koehler books are printed on long-lasting acid-free paper. When it is available, we choose paper that has been manufactured by environmentally responsible processes. These may include using trees grown in sustainable forests, incorporating recycled paper, minimizing chlorine in bleaching, or recycling the energy produced at the paper mill.

Library of Congress Cataloging-in-Publication Data

Names: Hall, Stacey, author.
Title: Selling from your comfort zone : the power of alignment marketing /
    Stacey Hall ; foreword by Sam Horn, CEO of The Intrigue Agency.
Description: First Edition. | Oakland, CA : Berrett-Koehler Publishers, [2022] |
    Includes bibliographical references and index.
Identifiers: LCCN 2021059162 (print) | LCCN 2021059163 (ebook) |
    ISBN 9781523001620 (paperback) | ISBN 9781523001637 (pdf) |
    ISBN 9781523001644 (epub)
Subjects: LCSH: Selling. | Sales management. | Customer relations.
Classification: LCC HF5438.25 .H3445 2022 (print) | LCC HF5438.25 (ebook) |
    DDC 658.8/1—dc23/eng/20220203
LC record available at https://lccn.loc.gov/2021059162
LC ebook record available at https://lccn.loc.gov/2021059163

First Edition
27 26 25 24 23 22   10 9 8 7 6 5 4 3 2 1
Book production: PeopleSpeak
Cover design: Susan Malikowski, DesignLeaf Studio

This book would not have come to be without the thousands of members of the sales and marketing industry who have tested my Alignment Marketing™ Formula and proven that more sales, satisfaction, and success are produced when we grow our business from within our comfort zone.

They are represented by these five winners of my contest to name this book. Next to their names are their top three core values, which form their comfort zone:

Enda Jones—honesty, respect, integrity
Rachel Rideout—honesty, love, freedom
Toni Taylor—wellness, integrity, authenticity
Joe Vular—integrity, authenticity, perseverance
Eric Yaillen—knowledge, honesty, integrity

My gratitude to each and all is everlasting.

Contents

Foreword

ONE OF THE SIGNS OF A GOOD BOOK is it stays with you.

Stacey Hall's book does just that. It causes you to question everything you thought you knew to be true about sales.

Many people are uncomfortable selling. They feel it is manipulative, coercive, a means to our end. Most salespeople are taught to *push* through this discomfort. They're told, "You've got to get *out* of your comfort zone if you want to succeed." The insinuation is that doing what doesn't feel right is somehow noble. The underlying message is that the more you get out of your comfort zone, the more you'll get used to it, and the better you'll get at it.

But what if that premise is wrong? What if the key to selling with integrity is to get *in* your comfort zone? What if the way to ethical influence is to clarify your core values and integrate them into your sales interactions so you feel good about what you're doing?

That's not idealistic—it's realistic. Ultimately, we're all in sales, so anytime we make a request or a recommendation, we're selling. We sell every day—at work, at home, online, and in public.

If we want to genuinely connect with people and make a positive difference, we will embrace this disruptive approach to persuasion and get *in* our comfort zone.

Get ready to go deep and take notes, and prepare to change the way you approach others and the way you do business.

The good news is when you get *in* your comfort zone and act in alignment with your core values, other people are more likely to respond in kind. And that's a win for everyone.

Sam Horn, CEO of the Intrigue Agency

Preface

My dad was in sales all his life, and I had a front-row seat to watch how the stress took a toll on him.

I watched him use the old-school tactics most sales trainers still teach today. With this approach, people are known as *targets*, which bothered my father. He enjoyed people. He enjoyed getting to know them. He was a good listener, always had a kind word, and did his best to find a solution to their problems.

He did not enjoy using the warlike tactics he was told to use. I know this because I grew up with the audio programs of these trainers playing in my home and when I was driving in the car with my dad.

He listened constantly and intently and attempted to do what the trainers and his sales manager told him to do. At the end of each day of making calls, this selling style did not sit well with him. The aggressive, win-at-all-costs approach was not in alignment with his nature.

It has never been with me either. That is why my goal in my career is to make sales in a way that feels good to both me and my prospects from the start.

If you have ever thought the following ideas to yourself, you are not alone:

- "Why am I being taught to expect constant objections instead of how to have my prospects want to say yes to me?"

- "Why do I have to go so far out of my comfort zone to do what my trainers, coaches, and managers are telling me to do to grow my business?"
- "Why is my sales team not achieving its sales quotas no matter how much training I give them?"
- "Why is it so hard to find good salespeople for my team?"

If you have these worries, you are in the majority of salespeople who are tired of disrespecting their core beliefs and who now refuse to use pushy and spammy sales approaches. More and more of them are leaving the sales industry for jobs that feel more purposeful and of service. This mass exodus is a shame because salespeople are meant to be solving problems, providing solutions, and helping make lives and businesses more successful. Salespeople can make a huge difference in the world!

If you are tired of spinning your wheels and wasting your time in dead-end cold-call conversations attempting to convince strangers that your products and services are exactly what they need, then it's time to get back into alignment—with yourself, your products and services, and your prospects. Too many people have problems that are not getting solved because you have been taught to use outdated, ineffective, old-school sales tactics that are instantly rejected.

Recent studies show sales training is linked to employee satisfaction, employee motivation, employee retention, sales results, company culture, and enterprise agility. Sales training that is not producing an increase in sales is having a negative effect on every aspect of a company.[1]

Now is the time for a more satisfying way to build relationships that result in sales. In this book, you will find a much more enjoyable and successful way because you will discover that your power and profit lies within your comfort zone—not by getting out of it.

I wrote this book for every

CEO
Vice president of sales
Sales director
Sales manager
Business development specialist
Account growth manager
Client engagement specialist
Inside sales account executive
Outside sales account executive
Marketing director
Marketing manager
Relationship manager
Team leader
Store manager
Retail sales associate
Customer service manager
Customer service representative
Telemarketer
Coach
Consultant
Author
Network marketing representative

This book is also for anyone who wants to become a better communicator and create healthy and productive relationships with others, including those with different personalities, cultural background, and opinions.

The tips and strategies contained here are designed to help you discover and keep you aligned with the following:

- Your core values, personal strengths, and sense of *purpose*
- Products or services you are selling and the company's mission
- Your audience and its needs and wants
- Solutions to your audience's needs and wants

You will also discover the Alignment Marketing Formula (Alignment + Belief × Consistency = Sales, Satisfaction, and Success), which has been proven to work by the thousands of people who are practicing this strategy to stay in their comfort zone to make sales, feel a greater sense of satisfaction, and achieve the success they desire and deserve.

Lastly, you will find a simple, easy-to-implement daily practice of maintaining your alignment and gently expanding the circumference of your comfort zone to avoid feeling overwhelmed as you attract and manage an ever-increasing amount of abundance.

I look forward to hearing that you, too, experience more sales resulting from stronger and more satisfying relationships with prospects who quickly become your customers.

I wish you an abundance of yeses every day, every week, every month, every year, and for all the years to come.

Why Your Comfort Zone Is Your Power Zone

One of my clients recently said her previous coach told her she "had to get out of her own way to be able to make a sale." We have all heard this advice as well and done our best to "get out of our comfort zone" to try to be successful doing something others have told us we "should" do. This book destroys this long-held myth.

For decades now, sales trainers have all been teaching methods of getting sales that primarily rely on being pushy and learning scripts on how to overcome objections. This approach has been used for decades to teach how to "control" a conversation.

For many people, this idea of controlling a conversation means "controlling another person," which produces feelings of anxiety, which then decreases the likelihood of a successful sale. This same approach has been described over and over by salespeople—and potential customers—as her inauthentic, pushy, and spammy."

In her article "Buyers Speak Out: How Sales Needs to Evolve," Mimi An recaps the results of HubSpot's 2021 Sales Enablement Report: "In an unaided, open text question asking respondents to describe sales, HubSpot Research found there is still a strong association with salespeople being overly pushy and aggressive."[1]

Being pushy is also one of the greatest fears of those in the sales industry because it requires them to

- Go against their natural way of building relationships
- Be out of alignment with what they have been taught about treating people the way they want to be treated
- Learn skills to help them be successful in risky and uncomfortable situations

Hundreds of articles have been written and countless studies have been conducted by psychologists, psychiatrists, doctors, and researchers that prove that taking stress-producing risks creates more anxiety.

These training techniques force salespeople to go outside their comfort zone. In doing so, they tend to feel they have to bend themselves out of shape, which causes them to be out of alignment with their core values.

Strong feelings of worry negatively affect self-esteem, which leads to a lack of confidence and a lack of sales. The fear of being pushy is also the reason for frequent turnover in the sales industry. No one enjoys feeling defeated and rejected over and over. That is why so many people quit after being trained in these spammy sales tactics.

Of course, we can remember a time we found a way to actually do what looked like getting out of our comfort zone. If we were lucky, we found we enjoyed it. But, we reached that point only because we simply found a way to expand our comfort zone, not leave it entirely.

As an example, I did something that looked like I was stepping beyond my comfort zone when I went snorkeling at the Great Barrier Reef. I am not a good swimmer, and I was incredibly uncomfortable and nervous—I had not done anything like that before. And yet I was not going to pass up the opportunity to see the coral and sea life up close.

In actuality, I did not go beyond my comfort zone. I simply expanded it a little bit by doing something I really wanted to do yet had not done before. I took a quick snorkeling lesson, and I stayed in close proximity to the tour guide to feel safer. I accomplished my goal of checking off an item on my bucket list.

You could compare the expansion of my comfort zone to the elastic band in a comfy pair of sweatpants, as my friend Koriani Baptist does. The waistband has some flexibility to give a little more room to grow and move when our waistline expands a bit. Our comfort zone is also like a rubber band. Each one is created with a specific circumference to perform its task. Because it has some flexibility, it has the capacity to expand a bit beyond that circumference and still be fully functional. However, if it gets bent out of shape or is expanded too far—meaning it goes outside its set comfort zone—it snaps, breaks, and is unable to perform the function for which it was created.

What do rubber bands and sweatpants have to do with selling? Everything!

The call is growing louder to end practices that feel pushy to prospects and customers and push salespeople to their breaking point. Our comfort zone's expandable circumference allows for personal and business growth. To support this fact, the article "Women in the Workplace: Why Women Make Great Leaders and How to Retain Them," released by the Center for Creative Leadership, refers to research that proves people prefer personally meaningful work that connects to their values, purpose, and work-life balance. According to the article, they want "a specific type of employment that social scientists refer to as 'a calling.' Callings are jobs that people feel drawn to pursue; find intrinsically enjoyable and meaningful; and see as a central part of their identity. Research shows that experiencing work as a 'calling' is related to increased job satisfaction."[2]

For this reason, you will find within this book a new and simple sales training—a process for gently expanding your comfort zone to stay flexible and resilient throughout the selling process, including in the face of customer objections, by remaining in alignment with your calling.

By attuning with your purpose, you will discover how to be in alignment with yourself, what you are selling, your prospects, and what you are saying to your prospects.

This is what I mean by "selling from your comfort zone," which I call "Alignment Marketing." This book will guide you through the Alignment Marketing Formula:

Alignment + Belief × Consistency = Sales, Satisfaction, and Success

This paradigm-shifting approach steers salespeople away from using pushy and spammy sales tactics, which are outside of your natural comfort zone. It instead teaches you how to bring meaning to your role as a salesperson by solving problems as the first step in building relationships with your prospects.

Using this formula, you will build confidence and find the positive energy needed to achieve your goals. The more motivated you are, the more likely you are to stay in action, allowing you to grow gently and stretch comfortably daily to achieve larger and larger goals without reaching your breaking point.

By working within and expanding your comfort zone—by being in alignment with your core values and personality traits—you will have more confidence, more energy, and more courage to achieve your goals, which greatly increases the likelihood of making sales, experiencing satisfaction, and achieving success.

I love the reaction Sam Horn, CEO of the Intrigue Agency, had when I told her about the Alignment Marketing Formula. She said, "It's how to shift from incongruent to the congruent, from what feels wrong to what feels right, what is uncomfortable to what is comfortable, what we do our best to avoid to what we welcome and approach, and from making sales poorly to making sales well."

To support you in staying in action, each chapter explains how to stay in alignment with yourself, your company, and your ideal audience or prospects.

You will create your personal alignment strategy following these steps:

1. Identify your unique strengths and your purpose (or calling) for representing the products and services you choose to sell.
2. Craft your personal brand that both aligns with your company's mission and yet identifies who you are, what problems you can uniquely solve, and who you want to serve (your ideal audience). This defines the circumference of your circle of alignment.
3. Develop your certainty and confidence of your ideal audience and the problems (also called *pain points*) they want someone to solve.
4. Locate and connect with the people who match your ideal audience profile—whether in person or online. With this new Alignment Marketing Formula, you will never again spam your friends and family. Even better, you will learn how to start conversations with people who have been waiting to meet you.
5. Spark emotionally compelling engagement with your ideal prospects—whether in person or online.
6. Transition the connection with your ideal prospects through the Know, Like, and Trust stages all the way to the sale and beyond to a long-term profitable relationship that continues to be mutually satisfying to you and your customers or clients.
7. Practice a daily routine of alignment to gently expand the circumference of your comfort zone to avoid feeling overwhelmed as you attract and manage an ever-increasing amount of abundance.

Over the many years I have been coaching thousands of sales representatives in using the Alignment Marketing Formula, my clients report the following:

- More sales resulting from stronger and more satisfying relationships with prospects who become their customers faster
- Greater job satisfaction
- Increased self-directed motivation
- Longer commitment to the same company and the company's mission

I had the pleasure of interviewing five of my clients about their experiences using the Alignment Marketing Formula to grow their businesses and teaching this formula to others too. You will discover quotes from each of them throughout this book to support you in practicing the exercises and tips I suggest. I introduce to you these five clients:

Koriani Baptist—Koriani is the founder of Keepin' Your Life Together Consulting, where she helps Black Christian mama entrepreneurs keep their life together so they can fulfill their God-given purpose with joy and ease.

Carolina M. Billings—Carolina is the founder of Powerful Women Today, a global community of highly influential women entrepreneurs and professional women who want to make a difference in the world by showcasing their voices, expertise, talents, experience, and passion.

Elisa Mardegan—Elisa is a social media marketing consultant who helps women marketers cut through the confusion caused by all the different marketing strategies available by providing them with a customized plan to make more sales quickly.

Stephanie Y. Oden—Stephanie is a life and business success strategist with a proven system of strategies and tools to help home business owners make sales while engineering a life they love.

Thierry Alexandre—Thierry helps makeup artists, entrepreneurs, and network marketers attract the best qualified leads so they can monetize their brand faster while having fun along the way.

The guidance in the book takes the guesswork out of prioritizing who is the most ideal prospect for your company's products or services, making it easy for you to know who is likely to say yes and direct your focus on those prospects faster, which leads to sales happening much more quickly and with greater satisfaction.

Your comfort zone is your power zone. Let's get back into alignment and make more sales!

PART 1

Are You in Alignment with Yourself?

TO HELP YOU DISCOVER THE INNATE PERSONAL POWER available to you within your comfort zone of your core values and personality traits, we will begin by challenging the commonly held stigmas, beliefs, and myths related to getting out of your comfort zone versus staying in it.

One such misconception is that those who do not get out of their own way are lazy or unmotivated and thus will never be successful.

In fact, greater evidence shows that the anxiety created by the risk of leaving one's comfort zone leads to procrastination and inaction due to the innate fight-or-flight response to stress.

We will also determine the circumference of your comfort zone and explore the Rubber Band Effect to identify how much flexibility you have to gently stretch and expand your comfort zone from within so you can grow and succeed on a larger scale without extending past your breaking point.

CHAPTER 1

How to Stop Selling Out on Yourself

ACCORDING TO A POPULAR MYTH about comfort zones, if you stay inside yours, it means you are stuck, lazy, or unmotivated.

The Problem

Most sales "gurus" will tell you that to make progress, you need to feel uneasy and stressed. They think you must reach a level of pain and discomfort that feels so bad you cannot tolerate it any longer, and only at that point can you make a change. They also say that when you have reached that level of stress, you will have increased focus, creativity, drive, and productivity. It is common to hear from these trainers that the brain is lazy and wants to keep you safe. Therefore, ignoring your mind and taking risks will show you what you are "really made of."

They insist that you must be pushy, assertive, and ready to deal with nos to be as victorious and successful as they are. They draw comparisons between sales and warfare to make their point. They believe no one wants to go into a battle, but it is necessary in business. After all, war does "make the man."

Their bottom line is this: "Without putting yourself in stressful situations, you can't be successful."

Fight-or-Flight Responses

Haven't they heard that stress, fear, and perceived danger produce fight-or-flight responses?

According to psychologist Carolyn Fisher, PhD, in an article for the Cleveland Clinic, "The fight or flight response, or stress response, is triggered by a release of hormones either prompting us to stay and fight or run away and flee. During the response, all bodily systems are working to keep us alive in what we've perceived as a dangerous situation." The article goes on to point out, "Living in a prolonged state of high alert and stress (when there isn't any real reason for it) can be detrimental to your physical and mental health."[1]

Common negative effects on the body and mind caused by the fight-or-flight response to stress and fear include the following:

- Increased heart rate and blood pressure
- Pale or flushed skin, possibly the feeling of being cold and clammy or hot and sweaty
- Heightened senses, possibly the feeling of being on edge or on your guard
- Foggy or altered memory
- Loss of bowel control

These responses to stress and fear will probably not result in greater confidence and productivity.

The fight-or-flight responses produced by the common sales training methods could be why those who are working on getting out of their comfort zone or out of their own way rarely are successful. Simply the fear of failure and the anxiety created by taking a risk is much greater than any possible rewards.

Debbie Mandel, author of *Addicted to Stress: A Woman's 7-Step Program to Reclaim Joy and Spontaneity in Life*, describes the problem this way: "Many of us are busy escaping from the deficits of our personality by trying to be something we're not." However, she warns, trying to change our nature causes stress: "Stress is so inflammatory and it's become the cause of all disease. *It zaps energy, creativity, and sabotages relationships.*"[2]

For example, Koriani Baptist told me that she considers herself a "zero in one hundred seconds flat" type of person. She explained, "When I get going, no one can usually stop me from accomplishing my goals. But I was stopped by hearing no over and over again when following the go-for-no approach I was taught by other sales trainers. When someone says no to me, I want to respect them. I felt that by doing what I was taught, I was not being myself, and it did not feel good. It felt phoney and cheesy."

Further, by focusing on our personal perceived deficiencies, we are creating mental health problems for ourselves.

Low self-esteem and dissatisfaction with our life leads to relationship problems, addictions, more anxiety, and depression, according to the National Alliance on Mental Illness.[3]

Can You Get Out of Your Own Way?

I did a survey of hundreds of entrepreneurs and asked how many feel it is important to get out of their comfort zone to be successful. The overwhelming majority agreed with that statement. What this tells me is that they bought into the myth that they must get out of their own way.

However, when I asked these same entrepreneurs how many are *willing to be out of alignment with their core values,* the response was 100 percent that they would *not* be willing.

Could this mean that their innate selves know that attempting to do or be something they are not creates internal conflict and angst? I believe so. How could people ever really get out of their own way? Only by going the way we are meant to go can we stay in alignment and be truly successful.

Perhaps those that tell us we must get out of our comfort zone actually are saying *"I can teach you to go only my way."* If it appears that they are successful in accomplishing something they have never done before, it is only because the amount they stretched was still inside their circumference of comfort. They were still in alignment with their values and calling.

The Solution

Tap into the personal power available to you within your comfort zone of core values and personality traits.

Power and confidence come from the feeling that we know what to do and that we can count on ourselves. We launch our actions from a familiar, safe, and secure place. Anxiety and stress in this zone are at minimum levels, making us feel free to move forward. In this zone, we already have a track record of success doing specific tasks and honing our skills. And we have been consistently doing those tasks because those activities are aligned with our core values and sense of purpose.

Koriani Baptist describes how using the Alignment Marketing Formula and staying in her comfort zone has made such a difference for her: "When you told me I could stay in my comfort zone and still be successful, Stacey, I felt relieved. I felt immediately that I could still be me and make sales and still feel good vibes being me—to still be respectful to myself and my prospects."

Another Source of Internal Satisfaction

When we feel confident that our skills can be a contribution to others, we discover another source of internal satisfaction. Already being good at previous tasks tells our mind that we are likely to be successful at new tasks that require similar experience. We are also willing to stretch just a bit more to accomplish these new, similar tasks because we expect to be successful.

Stephanie Oden describes the feeling of expanding while remaining inside her comfort zone. She says, "Expansion is required if there is something I must learn to do to fulfill my goal. As long as there is the little voice saying, 'I think I can,' then there is a small level of belief that I can do it—even if I don't do it right at the beginning."

We learn new activities quickly because they are already similar to those we have done in the past with success. Creating habits and routines inside our comfort zone is easier too.

Rhonda Britten, founder of the Fearless Living Institute, in an interview for WebMD, shares her views on staying in one's comfort zone to be more powerful: "I'm not interested in people getting rid of their comfort zones. In fact, you want to have the largest comfort zone possible—because the larger it is, the more masterful you feel in more areas of your life. Some people call it a rut. It's not a rut. It's our place of reprieve, where we can conserve our energy and not have to figure anything out. If you deny that you have a comfort zone or pretend that you don't need one, you'll be stressed all the time."[4]

Self-Satisfaction Contributes to Success

Mental health experts agree that the feeling of being self-satisfied improves our mental well-being. The sense of satisfaction allows our brain to release dopamine and serotonin into our system, which are known as the "feel good" hormones.

Some of the many positive mental symptoms reported when people feel a sense of satisfaction include the following:

- Improved mood
- Increased attentiveness and focus

- Increased productivity and creativity
- Improved analytical skills
- Increased motivation

These sound like factors that actually contribute to success! There are physical benefits too:

- Improved sleep, which contributes to all other physical benefits
- Improved digestion, which means no more eating our gut out with worries
- Strengthened immune system, which promotes increased productivity
- Longer lifespan and the desire to live and be productive longer

As an example of transforming stress into satisfaction, I often hear from my new clients that they have struggled for years attempting to adapt to other people's suggestions of how to schedule their time or stay organized. This stress and desire to do what other people tell us to do usually stems from childhood when our parents told us how to behave.

I encourage my clients to realize they are now in control of their own lives. It is important to stop trying to do things the way they are "supposed" to. I suggest to my clients that they play with, explore, and discover ways of managing their time and staying organized, which will give them more physical and mental energy.

Once they do, they find they are more productive and creative. They are no longer selling their own skills short; they are more likely to feel confident and powerful while selling their products and services.

CHAPTER 2

The Rubber Band Effect

IF YOU STRETCH A RUBBER BAND beyond its intended circumference, it will lose stability and ultimately snap. Humans react the same way.

The Problem

The phrase "I am reaching my breaking point" describes the Rubber Band Effect perfectly. It means we have been pushed beyond our safe comfort zone and we are ready to have an emotional or physical breakdown—or both. Just like a rubber band, once broken, we feel we are left dangling and unable to support anyone.

Another way of describing the breaking point is through Rhonda Britten's metaphor of a dartboard:

- The bullseye is our comfort zone.
- The next ring out is our stretch zone.
- The next one out from that is our risk zone.
- Go out beyond the risk zone and you wind up in your die zone.

The objective of the game, therefore, is to hit the bullseye.

The Solution

To achieve larger goals, gently expand the circumference of your comfort zone to the edge of its safe boundaries.

If you believe you have a purpose or calling, then you know how it feels both to be in alignment with yourself and to be stretched out of alignment with that purpose.

Consider that the boundaries of your comfort zone are actually your core values. Just as a rubber band is designed to expand only so far before it breaks, such is true of us humans. We must expand gently, and our safe and comfortable zone has a definitive boundary where we feel we are aligned within ourselves.

For example, simply telling introverts to come out of their shells and become more social and visible is not likely to produce immediate results unless they want to be more social.

Elisa Mardegan, a social media marketing consultant, network marketer, and affiliate marketer, told me that her first upline sponsor wanted her to go out and meet people in person. Doing so was outside her comfort zone, so she would not do it. Instead, she quit the company.

Later, she discovered how to meet people online. She then chose to represent a company that encourages its reps to use social media marketing. Elisa says she feels comfortable meeting people this way because she thinks both parties are on the same level. As a result, Elisa makes sales, enjoys job satisfaction, and creates success for herself every day.

An Example of Gentle Expansion

Here is an example from my own life of how I gently expanded the safe boundaries of my comfort zone by staying in alignment with my core value of self-accountability (knowing what I choose to be responsible for doing, being, or having).

As a child, I kept my thoughts to myself and stayed in the background out of the way. I was uncomfortable being asked questions. I did not want the spotlight on me in any way.

My favorite place in the world was my bedroom, where I read books and wrote my stories. I would do both for hours on end. One summer, I chose to be self-accountable to reading a certain number of books to win a prize in a book-reading contest, which meant even more time reading alone in my room.

My mother would force me to go outside to play with others because she was concerned about how much time I spent by myself. I did not enjoy my time with the kids in my neighborhood, and they did not seem to like me either. It was probably because I was physically weak and awkward. I was not good at group sports, so they did not pick me for their teams until the very end. The situation was always uncomfortable and caused me anxiety because they did not see me as an asset in any way.

Plus, every minute away from my books was a minute that I was not being self-accountable to winning the contest. When I was outside of my bedroom not doing what I loved, I felt like a fish out of water. I truly was like a rubber band bent out of shape, unable to do what I was designed to do.

These experiences as a child showed up in other areas of my life, and I was in constant fear of doing or saying the wrong thing when I was involved in activities with other people. I felt this way until it was time for me to choose a major in college. I chose to be self-accountable to have a job where I could write, travel, and help make a difference in the world.

At the time, a dear family friend was the head of the public relations department of a large electronics company. I had the opportunity to work with her for a couple of weeks one summer, and I fell in love with what she got paid to do every day.

I realized, though, to be successful in a job like that, I would have to learn how to be confident when interacting with other people. I chose to be self-accountable for gently expanding my comfort zone to learn how.

The good news about this type of career was I could still stay in the background as the one writing the articles. I would need just a little training on how to ask questions to gather information. Because I chose a career that was in alignment with my core values and sense of purpose, I was willing to stretch a bit within my comfort zone to learn this new skill of asking questions of others. I took some classes and little by little became more secure and confident.

I expanded my comfort zone further by taking classes in marketing, advertising, and radio and television production. I found easy ways to combine all those skills into a career with two Fortune 500 companies and a large prestigious university.

As I gained skills and confidence in those positions, I gradually felt my calling to be self-accountable in launching my own coaching and consulting firm to solve the marketing and sales problems so common among entrepreneurs.

To ensure I felt comfortable running my own business, I chose to be mentored for six months first. During that time, I was willing to play, explore, and discover in my stretch zone while learning the new skills required to be successful.

Throughout those months, I knew that if I felt I was close to the risk zone, I could either stop and go back to my comfort zone or I could get help from others to learn the new skills with less stress and anxiety. Sometimes I asked for and received that help.

I am pleased to say that I launched my own consulting business on the goal date feeling like I had hit the bullseye of alignment! Twenty-five years have passed since that day, and my sense of satisfaction grows daily, as do my sales and my success.

And by the way, I did win that book-reading contest!

CHAPTER 3

What Is the Circumference of Your Comfort Zone?

THE CIRCUMFERENCE OF OUR COMFORT ZONE is the place we feel safe. While in our comfort zone, we feel we were born to fulfill a purpose or were called to do something because we are a natural at it.

Identifying the Circumference of Your Comfort Zone

Our comfort zone is formed by our core values. Just like a rubber band, our comfort zone has enough flexibility to expand a bit to include a wider area. As we grow personally and professionally, take safe risks, and become more comfortable in various situations, our extended comfort zone also grows.

Within this range, we feel connected to and in alignment with our core values. This alignment creates the confidence needed to pursue our dreams. That confidence allows for more freedom in how to keep growing and improving our skills in harmony with our core values. Growth is much easier because we feel born to do whatever our calling is.

When Koriani Baptist first came to me for coaching on sales and marketing, I asked her to tell me about her core values. She replied that she had never been asked that question before. She later said, "I did not think of selling as having anything to do with what really mattered in my life. Selling was 'out there'—something separate from me. Once you asked me that question, I realized that selling and growing my business actually is all about me. And integrity is the key value for me, so everything I do in my business has to be done with integrity."

When Did Something Just Feel Right to You?

Take a moment now to think about a time when you wanted to learn how to do something you had never done before—for example, play a new instrument, write a book, quilt a blanket, or grow your audience on a social media platform—and you enjoyed the process.

You felt the *why* of what you were doing. You felt aligned with your purpose and calling as you mastered new skills and abilities. You could say it just felt right to expand in this way.

Finding the Edge of Your Comfort Zone

Take another moment and consider a time when you felt you *should* learn how to do something you had never done before. This could be a time when you procrastinated getting started. Perhaps you never fully mastered the new activity or skill because you could not see the point in moving forward toward its completion.

You may still be wondering why you never finished what you started. Perhaps you're beating yourself up for not finishing it successfully.

Then this may come as good news to you: what you discovered is that to move forward would have meant being out of alignment with your core values in some way. You found the edge of your comfort zone.

Fear Is a Warning Sign

During that experience, you may have felt you were getting bent out of shape by attempting to do what would be required to be successful. You may have felt anxious or worried, which caused you to slow down your progress forward because you were fearful about what was ahead if you continued in this direction.

Other people will tell you to face this fear if you want to be successful. I say fear is an indication that something about what lies ahead is outside our comfort zone—that we cannot see a way to remain in alignment with our core values and priorities. Fear tells us to check in with ourselves to make sure what we are moving toward is in alignment with our values and purpose.

If we discover that moving forward feels painful, we can trust that to go further in this direction will force us beyond our comfort zone. If we attempt to ignore and push past those feelings, we will reach our breaking point, when we feel we are under constant stress. We have lost our personal power and we no longer have the confidence in our ability to be of support to those we want to serve. We feel brittle and often snap, becoming useless to ourselves and others.

Why You Are Probably Not a Procrastinator or Perfectionist

Finding yourself stopped due to fear has nothing to do with being a procrastinator or perfectionist.

If you believe you fall into one of these categories, I am here to say that you likely expanded past your stretch zone where you were in alignment with your values. When you are stopped from moving forward, you can become lost without the internal compass of your core values to direct you toward how to feel safe, secure, and powerful again.

Our core values are our fundamental beliefs that guide our behavior and decisions. When our core values exert a strong influence in our lives, they are more powerful than our personality traits.

Psychologists Suzanne Smith and Raeann Hamon called values "appraisals of what is desirable, worthwhile and proper. Values lend meaning to life and help shape goals and provide direction."[1]

The Relationship between Core Values and Moral Values

Core values also have influence on our moral values, which govern our desire to be good. Moral values differ slightly from ethics: morals are the rules and ethics provide the motivation for our actions.

Here is an example of how our ethics, morals, and core values work together to keep us feeling safe, secure, and confident that we know what to do:

Ethics—You shouldn't lie to your customers.
Morals—Being honest is good.
Core value—Trustworthiness is important to you.

When we feel safe, secure, and confident, we are within our comfort zone. Furthermore, that confidence provides the power to stretch just a bit to expand and grow while remaining in alignment with our values.

I asked Rodolfo Rodriguez Jr., CEO of Virtual Event Sales Team, if he believed that being aligned with his core values helps him to be more successful. He replied,

The results I have in my life are a reflection of my core values. And different results come from which core values I honor at any given time. For example, I am successful in sales because two of my top three core values are contribution and growth. I believe things either grow or die . . . nothing stays stagnant. Happiness to me is seeing someone grow. I am passionate about teaching others to represent services that help other people to grow because I get to connect with my values.

Contribution and growth are the reasons we have achieved over $30 million in sales of coaching services over the past five years. Not a single day has felt like hard work. We find great salespeople because our interview process screens for people who value teamwork, integrity, and intelligence as well. I think that has contributed massively to the $30 million in sales.

He went on to explain that in another area of his life—financial investing—he lost a lot of money through bad decisions by investing in risky ventures. Once he chose to expand his comfort zone by adding being "intelligent with resources" as his fourth core value, his financial investments have been much more lucrative.

A List of Common Core Values

I have provided a list below of the most common core values.[2] As you read through it, ask yourself the following questions:

1. Which of these core values are in my top three?
2. Which core value is my most important core value?
3. Which of the core values on the list below is least important to me?
4. Are any of my core values missing from this list? If so, add them.

These questions have been designed to help you discover the circumference of your own comfort zone to ensure you know which core values are most important to you so you can make choices that are in alignment with these values.

Adventurousness

Animal care

Authenticity

Charity

Collaboration

Compassion

Consistency

Contribution

Cooperation

Courage

Creativity

Diversity

Efficiency

Emotional independence

Environmental care

Equality

Faith

Family

Fearlessness

Financial independence

Flexibility

Freedom

Friendship

Fun

Generosity

Growth

Health

Honesty

Integrity

Intelligence with resources

Joy

Justice

Kindness

Knowledge

Leadership

Love

Loyalty

Motivation

Open-mindedness

Optimism

Perseverance

Personal growth

Productiveness

Reliability

Respect

Responsibility

Self-accountability

Self-acknowledgment

Self-care

Service

Social responsibility

Spirituality

Transparency

Trustworthiness

Wealth

Wellness

Priceless in Its Value

Your list of core values is priceless. It is the source of your self-confidence and self-assurance. With this list consciously in your mind and heart, you will feel in control of your life because you accept and trust you know the direction in which to move forward. From this list you will draw courage and the motivation to slowly and gently expand your comfort zone to achieve ever larger personal and business goals.

Stephanie Oden shared with me her top three core values: loyalty, self-accountability and optimism. She told me that when she would meet people who were negative, she would do all she could to motivate and inspire them. She got tired and burned out from trying. She doesn't do that anymore because she found the Alignment Marketing Formula and realized that people who choose to be negative and require a babysitter to accomplish their goals are not her ideal audience. She now feels secure knowing she is meant to attract people who choose to be loyal, self-accountable, and positive and optimistic like her.

Elisa Mardegan revealed her top three core values are freedom, courage and family. When she first started in business, she did not consider whether what she was selling or whom she was selling it for were in alignment with her core values. It quickly became evident that the company she represented back then was not going to provide the support she required to build up her courage. They left her alone to do what was required on her own even though she did not know how or have the confidence to do it. She lacked the courage to go on by herself. She also realized the company did not give the same value to family as she did. As a result, she chose to stop selling that company's products.

Thierry Alexandre declared his top core values are freedom, respect/self-acknowledgment, and self-care/love. He puts his focus on them during his meditation first thing in the morning to feel aligned with them. He says it makes him able to navigate through his day in a more organic way. It feels easier to connect with his audience (his "people" as he calls them) and to be more intentional with his activities.

In upcoming chapters, you will discover how these people and others use their priority list of core values to make sales, have a deep sense of satisfaction, and stay in alignment with themselves to achieve success.

And so can you!

You will learn how to use the experiences you have of triumphing over life's challenges to authentically sell the products you represent. You will be able to make a difference in people's lives and be a beacon of hope for those you serve while feeling you are in control of your life and able to pursue your passion projects and enjoy a prosperous livelihood.

In the meantime, because you now know the order of importance of your core values, you can consciously make choices in any situation to stay true to and maintain alignment within yourself even while gently stretching to acquire new skills and experiences you choose to build.

You will also quickly know when you feel out of alignment. When you notice you are being asked to stretch in a new way that feels uncomfortable or dangerous, it will be a signal to check in with your core values. Do you want to expand your comfort zone by stretching in this way? Or would this stretch take you beyond your comfort zone and to your breaking point? Either choice now gives you control over how much you stretch at any given time. That control translates into personal power. And this personal power makes it possible for you to feel confident in fulfilling your goals from the safety and security of your comfort zone.

What Are Your Goals?

Before you consider your goals, take a look at a few sample goals that my clients have told me they want to achieve:

- To attract buyers daily who are ready to make a purchase
- To walk across the company's stage to receive an award for being a top salesperson
- To make a positive difference in people's lives and earn industry-wide recognition and respect
- To have the funds to buy whatever is needed and wanted at any time

Take a moment now to list your own goals—both business and personal. To determine your goals, consider these questions:

- Do you feel in alignment with any of the goals I listed above? If you do, how do these goals match your core values?
- If you don't, how would you adjust these goals so you can be in alignment with your core values?
- What other goals do you have that are in alignment with your core values?

By defining your goals in terms of your alignment with your core values, you will become more credible in the eyes of your clients. And from there, you can build a relationship with them.

PART 2

Are You in Alignment with What You Are Selling?

NOW THAT YOU KNOW THE CIRCUMFERENCE of your comfort zone, it is time to explore if what you are selling fits inside it.

Do you feel in alignment with the products or services you represent? Do you feel you can authentically and passionately speak about their benefits?

The more passionately in alignment you are with what you sell, the more credible you are to your prospects. In this section, I explain how that credibility will make it possible to sell faster and easier.

I will also invite you to consider ways you can create a satisfying and comfortable relationship with what you are selling by following the Know, Like, and Trust Principle. I will also guide you to identify your ideal audience—the people who you will want to get to know, like, and trust and who are likely to buy from you.

CHAPTER 4

Do You Believe in What You Are Selling?

RECENT STATISTICS PROVE more than half of all salespeople would do better selling a different product or service than the one they are currently selling or not selling anything.

The Problem

Herb Greenberg, Harold Weinstein, and Patrick Sweeney in their book, *How to Hire and Develop Your Next Top Performer*, correlated hundreds of thousands of assessments conducted over several decades. They found that 55 percent of people earning their living in sales should be doing something else. Another 20–25 percent have what it takes to sell, but they should be selling something else. An additional source found that 55 percent of salespeople don't have the right skills to be successful.[1]

I expect that a correlation exists between the facts that 55 percent should be doing something else *and* 55 percent don't have the right skills to be successful in sales.

Why Are Salespeople Unlikely to Be Successful?

These results invite us to ask the question, "Why is it that so many salespeople are unlikely to be successful?"

Sales experts attribute it to two factors:

- The company's recruitment and selection process
- The company reassigning employees to positions that do not match their skills

Both factors are related to the same root problem—confusion of strengths and skillsets—according to Tracey Wik, president and managing director of GrowthPlay's talent and organization effectiveness practice.[2]

The Responsibility Lies with the Salesperson

Sales consultants often give the responsibility for fixing the problem to the companies. They suggest a variety of personality tests and other means to clear the confusion during the hiring process and help a sales manager select the person with the right set of skills for the position.

I take a different view. I believe the responsibility lies with the salesperson.

Russ DeVan, the creator of the Success by Design Un-Training System, agrees with me as well. His program aims to make sales teams consistently productive. When we discussed this topic, he said, "Success happens by design, with structure and measured responsibility. We don't always get what we *want*, but we almost always get what we are *committed* to. And, we are always committed to something."

The only way the confusion will clear is when salespeople ensure that they are in alignment with what and how they are selling—and vice versa.

Following are three beliefs that most sales training programs are based on:

- "In sales, rejection comes with the territory. You will hear no, and you will hear it frequently. It's normal. What's important is what you do with that 'no.' "[3]
- "There's no lotion or potion that will make sales faster and easier for you—unless your potion is hard work."[4]
- "I like to think of sales as the ability to gracefully persuade, not manipulate, a person or persons into a win-win situation."[5]

If these beliefs are the basis for the sales training a company provides, and the salespeople do not feel their core values are in alignment with these statements, they will not excel at selling.

Alignment leads to belief. Belief turns into action—which is good news because that means this problem has an easy solution.

The Solution

Being aligned makes it easy to believe in what you are selling. I am inspired by what Jackie Sharpe, founder of Empowering Entrepreneurs Institute, shared when I asked if she agreed with my perspective: "First you have to believe in what you are selling. If you are not using the product or service you are selling, it is hard to speak from your heart. And you must speak from your heart in order to transfer your belief and your alignment to your prospects, as well as existing customers, friends, and especially potential business builders. That transference of belief and excitement is what creates the know, like, and trust factor with people, and with that, you can close more sales."

According to Amy Gallo, writing in the *Harvard Business Review*, the most successful salespeople have aligned their personal goals with work goals.[6] This indicates that salespeople who are in alignment with what they are selling are more optimistic and successful. That would make renowned sales expert Zig Ziglar happy. His body of work was based on his belief that success in sales requires belief in what you are selling.

Elisa Mardegan fully believes in what she is selling. As explained previously, she chose the company she represents based on staying in alignment with her core values. She says that her top value is "Freedom. . . . Everyone I have come across in my company wants time freedom and money freedom. . . . We are all on the same page. My company feels like a family. Everyone is helpful. I am free to be who I am and to speak how I want to speak."

By focusing first on how she wants to be of service in helping others experience more freedom, Elisa can cocreate soul-satisfying and financially satisfying relationships with her prospects.

Work as a Calling

The article "Women in the Workplace: Why Women Make Great Leaders and How to Retain Them," published by the Center for Creative Leadership, includes research that proves people prefer personally meaningful work that connects to their values, purpose, and work-life balance. They want "a specific type of employment that social scientists refer to as 'a calling.' Callings are jobs that people feel drawn to pursue; find intrinsically enjoyable and meaningful; and see as a central part of their identity. Research shows *that experiencing work as a 'calling' is related to increased job satisfaction.*"[7]

Norbert Orlewicz, business and marketing consultant and trainer and cofounder of MyLeadSystemPRO, believes this too. We had a conversation on this topic, in which he stated, "Sales can be a calling when it is an extension of a deeper purpose. When your business is aligned with your core values, you become passionate and transcend simply being a salesperson to become an *activist* with a vision, mission, and purpose for what you are selling."

Here are some optimistic and satisfying statements about sales:

- "Sales are contingent upon the attitude of the salesman, not the attitude of the prospect."[8]
- "People don't ask for facts in making up their minds. They would rather have one good, soul-satisfying emotion than a dozen facts."[9]
- "You don't close a sale, you open a relationship if you want to build a long-term, successful enterprise."[10]
- "Every brand isn't for everybody, and everybody isn't for every brand."[11]
- "Too often, sales reps simply regurgitate their presentations and expect to land the sale. It doesn't work."[12]

If the sales training provided by a company is focused on these statements and a salesperson is in alignment with these statements, he or she is more likely to take action toward making sales.

From Russ DeVan's perspective, "When we are committed to the value of a product or service, it is because we are aligned with it, and we feel congruent when promoting it. The courage of our commitment is felt as authenticity and passion. It is that authenticity that creates greater value for our prospects. And when value exceeds the cost, that is when our prospects say yes to buying what we are selling."

Confidence Produces Sales

Belief leads to action. And belief is grounded in being aligned with your core values, ethics, and morals. If you don't believe in what you sell—or you believe it can't actually solve your prospect's problems—then every time you are in a selling situation, you are facing an ethical dilemma, and that reduces your confidence that what you are doing is right and good.

Lack of confidence and alignment produces feelings of anxiety, which diminish your motivation to move forward. Your prospect can sense your lack of confidence and belief in your product or service. Even if you have learned the sales script perfectly, the difference in energy between someone who is confident and enthusiastic and someone who is not is obvious.

No confidence—no sales.

Alignment Produces Confidence

Kendra Lee of the KLA Group believes the top-producing salespeople are the ones "who radiate trust and confidence, and only make a recommendation when they honestly feel that their products and services can actually solve their prospects' problems."[13]

If your values don't align with the company's mission and values, you won't be motivated to expand your comfort zone when you need to learn new skills to be successful. This means you are not in alignment with how the company wants you to grow its client base and revenues. Your doubts, concerns, and fears will all be in your way, stopping you from doing what is required to make sales for that company.

Instead, you might procrastinate, as mentioned in chapter 3. You may do what is easy up until the point where your anxiety reaches the breaking point. And then you will do what more than 60 percent of salespeople do: leave the sales industry within three years because you are not making sales, experiencing satisfaction, or achieving success.

Let's get you back to your power zone—your comfort zone.

CHAPTER 5

Staying Inside Your Comfort Zone Increases Your Credibility with Your Prospects

IF YOU HAVE TO get out of your comfort zone to sell your products or services, then you have no authentic passion for what you are selling.

The Problem

Most people sell from their mind instead of their heart. Alignment is the connection from the heart to the ears to the mouth.

People are missing this pathway because they haven't taken the time to explore their core values. And they haven't noticed if their core values are in alignment with how and what they are selling. As a result, they have not created an emotionally satisfying experience for themselves with what they are selling.

Without a connection with your products or services—a personal passion for what you sell—you cannot be in alignment with your prospects. And without that alignment, you will have a much harder time making sales.

That was Stephanie Oden's firsthand experience. She said,

> I used to believe that I had to get out of my comfort zone to be successful because that is what I was first taught. I even used to teach my clients they had to get out of their comfort zone. Funny thing is, I didn't like doing it.
>
> Leaving my comfort zone puts me in a place of anxiety. I freeze up, and I feel like I am living someone else's core values. I give off an inauthentic energy. My prospects may not know what is not feeling right about talking with me. They may not realize I am not in congruency with my values. They can just feel that something is not working. And I don't make the sale.

Don't Lead with Logic

Shari Levitin, author of *Heart and Sell: 10 Universal Truths Every Salesperson Needs to Know*, provided a powerful explanation of this principle in a *Forbes* magazine article: "Whether you're selling dance lessons, real estate, software, or life insurance, remember that people buy based on emotion, and justify their decisions with logic after the fact. Show customers how good they'll *feel* as a result of using your product or service, and they'll buy from you today, tomorrow, and forever."[1]

If you cannot share your own personal story of how good your products or services make you feel—and what problems they have helped you and others solve—you have no authentic credibility from which to create alignment with your prospects.

Bernardo Tirado, an industrial psychologist, is quoted as saying, "Being authentic is the key to developing rapport, and people can sense a phony a mile away."[2]

Building a connection is based on likability, trust, and credibility. *No* credibility means *no* sales.

The Solution

Stay in your comfort zone, tap into your authentic passion, and increase your credibility with your prospects. Burning deep within each of us is our authentic passion, and it is powerfully attractive to others.

Passion Creates Compelling Credibility

Passion grows within us as a result of our experiences of living through personal triumphs and tragedies. Our authentic passion adds integrity and credibility into our words and actions. It is the emotionally compelling aspect that must be present in our interactions with our prospects if we want them to know how much we care about them and feel sure that our products and services can help solve their problems.

In many ways, salespeople are motivational speakers—whether talking one-to-one with a prospect or to a group of decision makers. To be effective in sales, we must learn to communicate with passion.

According to the ForbesSpeakers website, "Anyone can strive to be a speaker if they work hard enough, but passion and purpose will differentiate mediocre speakers from exceptional ones. With this, you are guaranteed to reach your audience while giving them something they can take away from it. This is not only important for your speaking career, but ensures that you will have a profound impact on others."[3]

Being Resourceful

If you are in the sales industry, you may have heard of Jim Britt, a renowned speaker, author of numerous best-selling books, and one of the world's top twenty success coaches.

You may not know he started his first entrepreneurial business with only nine dollars in the bank and borrowed four thousand dollars. A year later he had lost it all—home, both vehicles, furniture, everything.

But after that first year, with a lot of tenacity and a mentor, he turned the tables and shortly thereafter made his first million. He then started his speaking career as a business partner with the now late, great Jim Rohn for almost ten years, and Tony Robbins worked under his direction. Over the years, Jim has built a fortune worth millions of dollars with multiple streams of passive income from various business models.

Jim shared with me his secret for success and staying consistently passionate. He always feels "resourceful," which is one of his key core values. He explained that he had always had an affinity to the word *resourceful* and spent years meditating and reflecting on its various meanings. The first definition he found was "once again full of source." He then looked up the word *source*. It was defined as "where all things originate."

He continued his search for other definitions of *source*. Then one day, quite unexpectedly, he came across a very old dictionary in a small English village. In this book, the meaning given to the word *resourceful* was unique and struck a deep chord within him. The definition was "Love." So *resourceful* can also be defined as "once again full of love." He says, "When you set an objective to accomplish a certain thing, you actually fall 'in love' with it. Your only other option is to fall into fear. When you stay connected to what you love, you can accomplish the most amazing things in half the time."

How to Identify Your Authentic Passion

If you are not sure what your authentic passion is, you can start to identify it through these prompts:

1. What are all the problems and challenges you have had in your life? Make a list of them under these headings:
    - Growing a business
    - Looking more attractive

- Becoming healthier or more fit
- Becoming financially prosperous
- Being popular
- Improving the quality of your life

   Studies show that the majority of people around the world say these six categories are challenging to them.[4]

2. Which of the problems and challenges you listed above do you no longer have? Make another list of those challenges you have conquered. This second list is considered your area of expertise and credibility now. Congratulations! You found a way to stay in your comfort zone and be in alignment with your values to succeed in moving past a problem or challenge. This area is your authentic passion.

3. When you were going through each of the problems and challenges, what advice or help did you wish someone would have given to you? Add your answers next to each problem or challenge on your second list.

4. What lessons did you learn or what commitments did you make to yourself as a result of overcoming each of those problems and challenges?

5. If you met someone today who is now going through the same problems or challenges you overcame, what advice or support would you give him or her to help solve that problem?

6. If you had access to the product or service you sell now, how would it have helped you (or how does it help you) overcome your problems and challenges? In other words, how are your products or services in alignment with your core values in these categories?

Again, congratulations! You now have an emotionally compelling reason why you sell that product or service, which means you are in alignment with what you are selling. And you have an emotionally satisfying, authentic personal story to share with others who have the same problem or challenge.

But you actually now have more than just a story. You have a purpose, a mission, a satisfying reason for why you sell that product or service. You are no longer just a sales rep—you are now an authority and activist!

You can understand the pain of others because you have been there and you moved past that pain. That makes you a credible authority in this arena, someone others can look to for tips and advice. Even if you feel that you are not yet successful in moving past the pain, you can still be an authority by being honest with others that you are still in the process of learning how to overcome the pain, problem, or challenge.

Julie and Julia

For a good example of someone finding her purpose, let's look at the story behind the movie *Julie and Julia*, starring Amy Adams (who plays Julie Powell) and Meryl Streep (who portrays Julia Child, the famous chef).

Julie Powell is the author of the blog that inspired the movie. When Powell began her blog in 2002 she just wanted to write about her experiences of cooking every recipe in Child's *Mastering the Art of French Cooking*. She wrote to friends who then shared her blog and helped her attract a huge audience of readers who found her tales of mistakes in the kitchen and in her real life to be authentic and relatable.

Julie never claimed to be a great cook. She was truthful from the beginning that she started the project to "get a life." While she was not sure what her purpose was, she was sure she was being "called" to cook and write.

As described in a *Newsweek* article written by Jennie Yabroff about Julie, "She was miserable in her job, hated her apartment, and was losing faith in herself. She was desperate to be more than a housewife—she just didn't know what. Her earliest blog posts show that she was substituting and omitting, screwing things up and hoping a liberal application of butter would cover her sins. Along the way, she found herself."[5]

She began by telling her truth of being miserable and wanting to find her purpose. Along the way, she became known as an authority on managing life as well as French cooking. Her honest and authentic posts provided emotionally satisfying experiences for her readers.

She became an authority in finding one's self to her readers, who also wanted to be able to find themselves, so they kept saying yes to wanting to read her blog and ultimately her book, and they went on to seeing the movie.

A Powerful Purpose

Carolina M. Billings similarly found herself and then created the worldwide Powerful Women Today movement by staying true to her core values of emotional independence, financial independence, fun, and self-accountability.

For many years, Carolina was the CFO of multimillion dollar organizations, often the only woman at the top. And even more often, she was the only Latina at the top of these organizations. She often felt that she was the odd man out or had to work harder to fit in. She was told that she should change her personality, become more aloof to employees, and get an MBA if she wanted to get to the next level of success. After researching hundreds of MBA programs, she found a way to create a customized program that allowed her to have independence and fun and be self-accountable rather than having limitations imposed on her.

Later, she had a desire to improve other dynamics in her life and began looking for a community that would be a safe space for any woman leader to express her dreams and receive support and encouragement in achieving them. She could not find any that met her needs fully. Out of necessity she founded her own organization, Powerful

Women Today. It started as simply her passion project with a group of friends who wanted to take an action-forward approach to improve what was not working in their lives. It soon became her calling, mission, and purpose.

She left the corporate world to build Powerful Women Today full-time, and she says she is fulfilled because she is achieving goals within her own value system. The activities she now undertakes feel natural. She is able to show up as her authentic self.

She describes the difference between working within her comfort zone and working outside of it:

> Someone can be proficient working at something that is outside their zone of values. However, it will take more energy and more effort. Work feels like work; it doesn't feel "right" on some level, and you will pay the bill at some point. Yet when working from within your comfort zone, we are playing to our strengths and can easily "go the distance."
>
> Traditional sales training will only fit one-quarter of the population. Even if 100 percent try, it will be received by only 25 percent of the population. We must let birds be birds and fish be fish and not expect birds to be fish or vice versa.
>
> We must encourage people to validate, respect, and honor each person's comfort zone as the core of diversity and inclusion. As a Hispanic in Toronto, although a metropolitan city, I may be the only person that looks like me in a restaurant or in meetings. As I became more aware, I also became more confident in my thought leadership. For example, I was invited to attend what was called a Global Economic Forum. Of the thirty-six speakers, thirty were men, of which two were nonwhite; the six women were each white.
>
> I respectfully replied to the organizers and expressed I felt the responsible thing to do was to decline the invitation to attend due to the lack of diversity. I supported my decision with data and statistics related to diversity and inclusion.

Staying aligned with my values, I feel comfortable in my own skin to speak my truth and choose to highlight ways that others can be more inclusive too. That is how I attract members and grow Powerful Women Today.

Carolina M. Billings was willing to face the challenges she experienced, and she has turned them into a triumph.

A Passion Can Lead to a Purpose

Sometimes a person may not want to revisit the problems and challenges they have faced in life because they are too painful. If you are one of those people, you can ask yourself the following questions instead:

- What are your interests and passions?
- What makes you happy?

Perhaps you are passionate about knitting and would enjoy sharing your knowledge and knitting tips with others, or you are in the process of learning to knit. Or you love to work out or are just starting a workout regime. Consider how the product or service you sell helps you enjoy your interests that much more and provides an emotionally compelling reason for why you sell that product or service.

For example, people who just started a workout regime are actually an authority on starting to work out. Here are a few ways they can use their passion to find their purpose:

- They could sell nutritional supplements because the supplements help them have a more productive workout.
- They could sell athletic wear because they like the way they feel in the clothing.
- They could sell coaching services because it allows for scheduling their workday around their workout schedule.

- They could even sell travel services if they want to visit different gyms all over the world.

Remember, a wide variety of products and services are now able to be sold through a multitude of home-based and direct-sales companies. For example, you could sell insurance, retirement plans, travel services, nutritional supplements, or products that make it possible for grandparents to spend more time with or take better care of their children and grandchildren.

Give Value to Your Personal Experiences

Norbert Orlewicz feels strongly that our own personal experience is the most valuable source of credibility—which is when we believe in ourselves and others believe what we are saying to them. He said, "Most people don't value the experience they have gained through life. Personal experience is ten times the value of academic knowledge. Any lack of knowledge can be made up for with experience. Get out there and do it and keep learning in the trenches. Become a 'specialist' or an authority in what you know because of your personal experience. You will become known as someone who 'knows what they are talking about' in the areas your ideal audience wants to learn."

By matching what you sell to your authentic passion based on your personal experience, your connection with your prospective audience will be built on a solid foundation of authenticity and credibility.

CHAPTER 6

The Know, Like, and Trust Principle Produces Sales

Since sales is based on relationships, if prospects do not first know and like you, they will not trust you. To sell requires trust.

The Problem

Unfortunately, decade after decade, sales training programs teach to sell first and then build relationships later. This approach is the same as seeing a stranger on the street whom you find attractive and asking him or her to marry you—without so much as asking to meet for coffee first. It is not beyond reason to expect that if you meet enough strangers, you might find a person who is lonely or curious enough to say yes to you. Time and time again, though, you will be told no.

Sometimes instant connections can happen. You may bond over a mutual love of dogs or a portfolio case—yes, that really happened to me. Someone liked the style of my portfolio case and offered me a job, which I accepted and enjoyed immensely. The next thing you know, you are talking daily about something of interest to you both. But most often it takes time.

The Solution

Building a strong connection with another human being that is soul-satisfying and comfortable to you both is a natural process. During this process, you are trying to identify if you are in alignment with each other's core values and if you fit into each other's comfort zones.

The Know, Like, and Trust Principle

Creating a close and trusting connection takes time—a lot of time, in fact, according to a 2018 study on personal relationships.[1]

While making connections through social media can happen much more quickly, all strong relationships—especially those that result in consumer loyalty—must develop through the Know, Like, and Trust Principle.

The Know Stage

At the Know stage, we first introduce ourselves to the other person. The relationship needs to start slowly. During this stage, it is important to disclose something meaningful about ourselves and see if our new friend or prospective customer will do the same.

The Like Stage

At the Like stage, we find out if we are in sync. Are we in alignment with each other's core values? Is what we are selling likely to solve the other's problems and meet his or her needs?

During this stage, it's important to lighten up, explore, and allow the exchange of authentic thoughts and feelings. This allows our prospective customer to develop a sense of being safe with us. Experience this stage as an opportunity of discovery.

Do not start asking for a purchase at this stage. Not enough trust has been built yet. During this stage, we want to demonstrate we are trustworthy.

The following are some ways both parties can demonstrate their trustworthiness according to psychologists:

- Honor and keep your own commitments and agreements.
- Clearly communicate requests when making agreements.
- Have realistic expectations instead of greedy desires.
- Have the courage to say no when something is not in alignment.
- Maintain your strong boundaries while showing empathy to the other person.
- Tell the truth about your actions and feelings.
- Admit mistakes and solutions for correcting them.
- Be positive, calm, and confident.
- Listen carefully to the other person, and respond promptly and appropriately with respect and consideration.
- Offer support and ideas rather than self-promotions and product advertisements.
- Provide multiple channels of communication for ease of access (phone number, email, social media sites, etc.).[2]

Remember this adage: nobody cares how much you know until they know how much you care. During the Like stage, it is essential to consistently demonstrate how much we genuinely care for the other person.

Most importantly, we should be asking questions of our prospects.

Walter Aguilar, president and owner at Power vs Force Coaching, shared his viewpoint me with me: "Sales is a value exchange. I ask questions to identify if the values of my prospects are in alignment and congruent with my own and if I can give them what they want in exchange for what I want. I let them know upfront that I don't know if we will be a good fit for each other, and then I lead them through an assessment process so we can both find out."

The Trust Stage

We arrive at the Trust stage through being consistently reliable in practicing the activities suggested during the Like stage. As the salesperson, you have a right to expect your prospective customers to practice these trust-building activities too. As Albert Einstein said, "Whoever is careless with the truth in small matters cannot be trusted with important matters."[3]

Building trust requires both parties be able to live within the same comfort zone circumference—satisfyingly in alignment—with neither one being bent out of shape to be in a relationship with the other.

Understand and apply the *Know, Like, and Trust Principle* to make sales inside your comfort zone.

The Build, Engage, and Sell Process

According to Rare Consulting, "86 percent of consumers say loyalty is primarily driven by likability and 83 percent of consumers say trust."[4]

In the marketing world, the terms that correspond to know, like, and trust are build, engage, and sell.

Know = Build your audience
Like = Engage with your audience
Trust = Sell to your audience

Build Your Audience (Know)

Audience refers to your soon-to-be leads, prospects, and customers (or clients, patients, or team members). To build your audience means to meet people who match your ideal audience, the people you believe you can help.

To meet them first requires knowing the profile of your ideal audience. I said *ideal* audience and not *target* audience or *avatar* for a specific reason. The definition of a *target* is "a person, object, or place selected as the aim of an attack." The use of this term in marketing circles gained popularity with a certain approach to sales based on warfare tactics. Personally, I do not find warfare tactics satisfying, comfortable, or relaxing. If you do, then it's best to put down this book and choose one that shares how to apply aggressive and defensive strategies to be able to "win" sales battles.

Regarding the use of *avatar*, which according to Lexico.com means "an icon or figure representing a particular person in video games, internet forums, etc.," I prefer to remember that I am interacting with a real person. Referring to potential customers as avatars is an easy way to dehumanize them, which makes it easier to not care about their feelings and problems.

In this book, I refer to our audience as ideal because they are. We know the problems our ideal audience wants solved—and we have the products and services to solve them. Those people in our ideal audience zone are in alignment with us, and vice versa.

Engage with Your Audience (Like)

In addition to all the activities to practice in the Like stage already mentioned, to engage with your audience from a sales perspective means creating valuable content in a variety of ways to serve your audience. Valuable content solves the problems of your audience in an emotionally and mentally satisfying way.

When your content reaches that level, they will want to engage with you by commenting and responding. As you acknowledge and respond back, you are demonstrating that you sincerely care about them. In part 3, I provide examples of how to create emotionally and mentally satisfying content. For now, let's focus on the importance of acknowledgment—as the most valuable content you can offer.[5]

Acknowledgment is defined as "the act of recognizing the existence of someone or something" and is a powerful recognition of the whole person. This act is important because in our fast-paced, no-time-to-think world, the majority of people feel unappreciated, taken for granted, and unseen. Despite being more connected than ever through social media, a recent survey of more than two thousand American adults found 72 percent report having felt a sense of loneliness, with nearly one-third (31 percent) experiencing loneliness at least once a week. Jennifer Candle, DO, notes, "Long working hours, increased use of social media—in many cases surpassing in-person interaction—and a mobile workforce traveling or living far from family contribute to the high rates of loneliness."[6]

An experiment to test the importance and quality of acknowledgment was done in Japan. Families placed three jars of rice and water by their front door. Each morning and night they would say, "I love you," to the first jar and "You fool," to the second one. They ignored the third jar completely. After a week, the first jar began to ferment and grow, the second jar started to turn black, and the third jar they had ignored was totally dead.[7]

This experiment has a direct application to people around the globe. It became even more apparent during the COVID-19 pandemic and subsequent lockdowns that people are craving social interaction more than ever.

This offers an opportunity for those of us in sales who can fulfill this need for connection—whether meeting in person or choosing to build an audience through social media.

Sell to Your Audience (Trust)

Trust is built through the presence of these five factors in a relationship: consistency, an exchange of value, mutual benefit, truthfulness, and acknowledgment.

Consistency—Both parties do what they say they will do consistently and dependably.

An exchange of value—Both parties provide the value expected—or more value than expected—to the relationship.

Mutual benefit—The relationship is equally beneficial to both parties.

Truthfulness—Both parties are honest and authentic with each other.

Acknowledgment—Both parties recognize each other's accomplishments and emotions.

The Winning Formula in Sales

By combining the Know, Like, and Trust Principle with the Build, Engage, and Sell Process, you have a winning formula for making sales easier and faster.

Koriani Baptist described to me the difference that combining them has made in her ability to grow her business and make more sales:

In the past, when I would go live on my social media sites, I was attempting to reach as many people as possible, anybody who would watch! I was getting views—sometimes hundreds of views—but no one was commenting or engaging with me, and I was not making any sales.

Once I started to combine the Know, Like, and Trust Principle with the Build, Engage, and Sell Process, I realized I could stop selling to the whole world like others taught me to do. I could focus in on my ideal audience of Black Christian Mama Entrepreneurs— women of faith who feel stressed out by racism, by being a woman and a mom, and also by working from home. They are who I was!

And knowing how they feel because I felt that way in the past made it easy to know where to find them, what to say to them, and how to relate to them. I felt confident that I have the "stuff"—the goods—that this audience wants.

Now when I go live or share a post, I talk about one of the problems this audience is facing, such as feeling overwhelmed, having no time for themselves, not feeling worthy to be a business owner, or experiencing parenting challenges. And I invite them to come to a private group I created for people who fit my ideal audience profile to get the solutions. I no longer just give the solutions away to just anyone.

In my private group, I build relationships with the members. I am not presenting myself as someone with just academic credentials. I authentically share my own personal experiences and solutions that have worked to solve problems similar to theirs. By sharing my truth, it sparks engagement. That engagement leads to a sense of trust with me. When I then offer something they can purchase—a product or coaching program for example—they buy it because they already know, like, and trust me. They know I am going to help them take the shortcut out of the problem and direct to the solution.

Their interest in what I have to say has increased my confidence, clarity, and feelings of worthiness. I now expect—rather than hope—I will receive an exchange for the value of my knowledge. I know that people who match my audience will pay for the value I provide.

Trust Is Built through Consistent, Positive Engagement

Author Colleen Francis agrees that acknowledgment is a key ingredient to engaging with our audience if we want to build trust in the relationship. She writes, "To acknowledge someone is to say: I see you. You are significant. I understand you . . . I admire you. This is the case with all humans, and because all selling is ultimately Human to Human selling we need to pay attention to acknowledgment and use it everyday [*sic*] to help us sell more, in less time."[8]

The everyday practice of acknowledging people who engage with us as an important element in creating trust during the sales process is reinforced by the *Harvard Business Review*, which conducted a series of studies on the topic. The research proves acknowledging the emotions of others can foster trust. The act of verbally recognizing people's feelings is perceived as an effortful act and can help form deeper connections with them. But, when acknowledgment is seen as being motivated by selfish reasons—with an ulterior motive—it is not as effective.[9]

Ask Thoughtful Questions

One of the key engagement activities and an effective way to show acknowledgment is to ask thoughtful questions and carefully listen to the response, which demonstrates an interest in truly connecting with the person.

Jim Britt, success coach and best-selling author, has become successful by doing just this. He starts every conversation with "How are you?" and then listens intently for what he can do to help. And he keeps asking his prospects questions to determine the following:

1. Do they have a pain or problem?
2. Do they want to solve the pain or problem?
3. Can he help solve the pain or problem for them?

Be Responsive to Requests

Being responsive to requests is another way to show acknowledgment and build trust. A study shows customers are willing to spend up to 20 percent more money on an item from a business that responds to their customer service tweet.[10] Another study reports 73 percent of customers say time is an important factor in distinguishing a good customer service experience from a poor one. Speed in both response and resolution are at the top of the list of most desired qualities in a customer experience. [11]

Show Respect

If you want to build trust even faster, make sure you use your customers' names with respect. The well-known adage "Nothing is as beautiful to a person as the sound of his or her own name" is especially applicable when making sales. Yet, the amount of carelessness shown with people's names is simply astounding. My name is often misspelled in communications, even when the correct spelling is provided by the social media site (for example, in Facebook Messenger).

Another mistake people make with my name is automatically calling me Stace instead of Stacey. Someone who calls me Stace before I have truly reached the stage of trusting them will rarely make it into my comfort zone. This too-familiar way of using my name—without asking me what I prefer—immediately shows me that I am not in alignment with the person. Even my husband, Bill, doesn't call me Stace and never has. Stace is the name my father called me, and it is a precious reminder of him for me and therefore is much too personal a name for a new acquaintance to use.

Always make it a practice to ask people what name they prefer to be called. If you do not know how to pronounce the person's name, ask for instructions. Don't try to pretend that you know. It just makes you look like a fool and a know-it-all. And who likes a know-it-all?

The Right Time to Ask for the Sale

If you engaged well and discovered where you and your prospect align, you are now ready to offer your products and services. At this point your prospects are likely to say yes to you because they trust you. They feel you have their best interests at heart and believe in what you believe in. If you like the product or service, they believe they will too. Now it's time to ask for the sale—and not before this moment!

Scripts aren't necessary to overcome objections. You will not likely hear an objection at this point. You do not need to put on your battle armor because there is no war. You and your prospects can stay in your personal comfort zones, and they will make a purchase from you.

Most people in sales don't ever get to experience this moment because they started selling (also called pitching) as the first step, hoping to get the person to respond and lastly hoping to eventually build a long-term relationship with the prospect. Doing sales this way is what gets good people labeled as pushy and spammy.

Don't sell yourself short by selling to your prospects too early. Follow the Alignment Marketing Formula, and you will ultimately arrive at the satisfying destination where your prospects say yes to you.

I will even share with the you the exact twenty-seven-word phrase I ask to help me determine if the time is right. You will find it in chapter 12.

Resist the urge to fast forward to that chapter. The guidance and suggestions offered in each of the chapters leading up to that chapter are essential to master or the phrase won't work for you as it does for me. And I get a yes far more times than any other answer once I ask it of a prospect.

So, don't rush the Alignment Marketing Formula if you want it to help you make more sales too.

Why Does It Take Time to Make a Sale?

Building relationships that will ultimately end in a sale will take some time. That is often why other sales gurus will preach to reach out to your "warm" market of people you know to get sales faster.

But often the people we know are already our customers or clients or they have no need for what we are selling. And we may have already reached out to them—more than once—and they have already said no. For these reasons, I tell all my clients at the beginning that if you don't have the time to build a friendship, you don't have time to be a successful salesperson.

If you are desperate for money, you may have to get a job and save up until you can afford to sell what you really want to sell and serve the audience you really want to serve.

The Alignment Marketing process starts slowly, yet it quickly builds momentum and snowballs into meeting a multitude of people who will become your friends and then your team members and clients. The key is being consistent daily.

The New ABCs of Selling

The old ABCs of selling were known by the phrase "Always be closing." Is it any wonder that salespeople are considered pushy and spammy? This idea is not based on consistency or alignment.

Consider the new ABCs of selling: alignment, belief, consistency.

Each one is a key element in the Alignment Marketing Formula:

$$Alignment + Belief \times Consistency = Sales, Satisfaction, and Success$$

The alignment stage of the formula is where we combine the Know, Like, and Trust Principle with the Build, Engage, and Sell Process. I will explain how to use this formula to your advantage in the following chapters.

Carla Archer, a marketing consultant to fitness professionals, shared her experience with the Alignment Marketing Formula:

> I was told by a company I was training with to get out of my comfort zone and do the sales activities they taught us to do. I was able to do those activities and I made sales, but it didn't feel right to me. In fact, it felt icky. I didn't feel I was presenting my true self. I felt the approach was mechanical and lacked caring. Rather than making a real connection with each person, I repeated a script. There was no time to get to know the person, so there was no way for me to personalize what I was saying to them.
>
> Using the Alignment Marketing Formula, I now show up as myself every day, I stay in alignment with my core values, I make real connections with prospects, and I serve my clients exactly the way that feels good to me to serve them.

Let's get started with how to get to know who your ideal audience is—the people who are already aligned with what you want to sell—so you can be satisfyingly successful too.

CHAPTER 7

Who Do You Want to Get to Know?

WHEN 55 PERCENT OF PEOPLE are selling the wrong product, this means that they are not in alignment with the product or service they are selling. They don't have an emotional connection to it, or they don't have a personal reason they believe in it.

By becoming in alignment with what you are selling, you become in alignment with all the people who want to buy what you are selling. That connection will make sales happen more often and quicker.

Selling from Your Mind versus Sharing from Your Heart

Salespeople who are not in alignment with their product or service wind up selling from their mind instead of what is in their heart. Alignment is the connection from the heart to the ears to the mouth—and they don't have it. As a result, they are not able to create an emotionally satisfying experience for their leads and prospects, so they can't sell their product or service.

People don't buy based on facts. They buy based on how they feel and back up the decision with facts.

Before you can be in alignment with a product or service—and the people who will want to buy that product or service—you must be fully honest with yourself in answering the questions I asked in chapter 5:

1. What are all the problems and challenges you have had in your life?
2. Which of these problems and challenges do you no longer have?
3. When you were going through each of these problems and challenges, what advice or help did you wish someone would give you?
4. What lessons did you learn or what commitments did you make as a result of overcoming each of those problems and challenges?
5. If you met someone today who is now going through the same problem or challenge you overcame, what advice or support would you give him or her?
6. If you had access to the product or service you sell now, what are all the ways it would it have helped you (or how does it help you) overcome your problems and challenges?

For an example of how this can work, let's look at Elisa Mardegan, who provides social media marketing consulting services to women entrepreneurs confused by all the different marketing strategies available to them. She says she was just like them at one time. Once she discovered the Alignment Marketing Formula, she went through the questions above and listed all the advice she wished someone would have taught her when she was just starting out and feeling the same confusion. Back then, she wanted someone to show her the shortcut through the confusion to be able to make sales faster.

Since no one had been there for her back then, she had to learn how to achieve her goals herself. Today, she knows exactly each step to take. By listing all the tips and wisdom she gained, she now has a coaching program she offers to prospects who match her ideal audience. She is in complete alignment with what she sells.

An Emotionally Satisfying Reason

If your product or service would have helped or currently helps you overcome your problems and challenges, you have an emotionally satisfying reason why you sell that product or service. This means you are in alignment with what you are selling. You are also in alignment with the people who will want to buy what you are selling.

When we share our personal stories of going through the same experiences, we become more trustworthy faster to our prospects who are dealing with the same issues. They feel our sincerity when we say our products or services will help them.

As mentioned also in chapter 5, if you choose not to revisit the problems and challenges you have faced in life because they are too painful, then use these questions instead to discover what you could sell that is in your comfort zone and aligned with your core values:

- What are your interests and passions?
- What makes you happy?
- What could you teach someone else to do?

If you are passionate about knitting and would enjoy sharing your knowledge and knitting tips with others, or if you are in the process of learning to knit, you could sell knitting supplies.

If you love to work out or are just starting a workout regime, you could sell fitness equipment, athletic wear, gym memberships, or nutritional supplements.

Maybe you are a grandparent who loves your grandchildren and enjoys sharing stories about them with other grandparents. You can offer products that make it possible for grandparents to spend more time with or take better care of their children and grandchildren.

Make Them Feel Valued

Consider how the product or service you sell helps you enjoy your interests that much more and provides an emotionally compelling reason for why you sell that product or service.

Sales is nothing more and nothing less than building relationships in which both people have their needs satisfied. As Walter Aguilar says, "Give value in exchange for what you want." If we accept this truth, then it's also important to accept that people do business with people who make them feel valued. They do not want your product, service, or offer (chances are thousands of marketers are also trying to sell the same product as you)—they want you! You understand the problems or interests of a group of people (your ideal audience), and you have solutions they definitely want.

Give Them Solutions

Become someone they want to know and follow. The more valuable information and experiences you provide—over and above the products and services you sell—the more money you make.

You may be thinking, "Okay great! This Alignment Marketing approach makes sense. But how do I attract customers and buyers to me, especially if I'm brand new or haven't made any money yet?"

The good news is that your prospects just want to know you understand their problems and you have the solutions. They don't care if you have been with your company for ten years or ten minutes. To quote

Norbert Orlewicz, "It's not about credentials; it's about how much you care about their needs and problems!"

This cannot be stressed enough. When you know whose problems you can solve, attracting your ideal audience and knowing the questions to ask so they understand how much you care about them becomes so much easier. As a result, you make sales happens faster.

Let's move on now to part 3, where we will be exploring how to let them know how much you care.

PART 3

Are You in Alignment with Your Prospects?

MAYA ANGELOU SAID, "I've learned that people will forget what you said, people will forget what you did, but people will never forget how you made them feel."[1] And Theodore Roosevelt told us that "Nobody cares how much you know, until they know how much you care."[2]

No matter who said it first or best—this is certainly true of sales.

Your sales training may have taught you to get straight to the point and offer the products or services as fast as possible so as not to waste your time or the prospect's time. This "me-me-me" approach gives the sales industry a bad reputation.

In this section, I demonstrate just how important it is to take the time to ask your prospects questions to first determine the extent to which they are aligned with you and vice versa. This practice is the Know, Like, and Trust Principle in action.

According to Robert Keith Leavitt, "People don't ask for facts in making up their minds. They would rather have one good, soul-satisfying emotion than a dozen facts."[3] To be someone who creates soul-satisfying emotional connections is to be willing to be authentically vulnerable and show empathy. Empathy is created by sharing how you, or someone you know, have experienced similar challenging situations and how your products or services solved the same problem. This level of empathy leads to sales.

When discussing this concept with Sam Horn, CEO of the Intrigue Agency, she shared her perspective: "Empathy means asking ourself, 'How would I feel if I was in this person's shoes?'"

How comfortable are you in being vulnerable? Is empathy one of your core values? In this section, I will ask you questions to help you know how prepared you are to build relationships that result in sales.

I will also help you discover exactly where you will find people who match your ideal audience profile and how to start a relationship with them that results in sales, satisfaction, and success.

CHAPTER 8

Do They Know How Much You Care about Them and Their Problems?

PEOPLE DON'T CARE HOW MUCH you know about your products or services because they don't need another product or service. What they need is a solution to their problems.

The Problem

Whether it was Theodore Roosevelt or Maya Angelou who said it best, the fact remains that nobody cares how much we know. They care most about how much we care about them, not about how much we know. Remember this principle when building any relationship. I will continue to return to this idea in the remaining chapters because it encompasses the most important principle to remember when building a relationship with prospects: they only want to know you care that they have a problem and they want to know you have the solution.

If you are not able to relate on an emotional level to a prospect's problems and if your product or service does not provide a direct solution to the prospect's problems, you will not make the sale.

As David Meerman Scott, business growth strategist and *Wall Street Journal* bestselling author of twelve books, including *The New Rules of Marketing and PR*, said, "What your buyers do care about are themselves. And they care a great deal about solving their problems (and are always on the lookout for a company that can help them do so)."[1]

The Me-Me-Me Approach

Most companies and salespeople use a me-me-me approach, which sounds like this: "Hi. Nice to meet you. Let me tell you all about me because if you see how great I and my products are you will want to buy them."

Right out of the gate all the attention is focused on the salesperson, the company, and the products or service. I am sure you have been the recipient of a me-me-me approach more than once.

When Is a Gift Not a Gift?

The most blatant recent example of the me-me-me approach I received was on my birthday. A network marketer whom I do not know sent me a private message wishing me a happy birthday. That was nice of her, right? Wait for it.

She invited me to visit her website and pick out "a gift for myself." I visited the website, I found something I liked, but I could not figure out how to receive it as a gift. I wrote her back to let her know and get the instructions of how to receive my gift. I received this reply: "I am not gifting you with anything. I thought you might want to buy yourself something from my website to treat yourself for your birthday."

Really? I didn't know her at all, but she was trying to use my birthday to pitch her products to me under the guise of asking me to spend my own money to "treat" myself. That was the very definition of a me-me-me approach.

And, yes, I let her know that I would not be buying anything from her in the future, so she could remove me from her list.

Me-Me-Me Social Media Messages

The majority of brochures, emails, and social media posts show "beauty" photos of the product, or people enjoying the product or service. The information is focused on the product or the service—how great it is, how new it is, how different it is to other similar products and services, and so on. Little is ever mentioned about the actual problems that the product or service is meant to solve or what type of people have that problem.

For example, within moments of opening my Instagram newsfeed one day I saw a post from a sales representative about a skin-care product (the name of the product has been changed to protect the guilty). The photo in the post showed three jars of the skin-care product. No people were included in the photo to give an idea of the type of person for whom the product is created.

The opening line of copy was "Today we will be discussing the body trio! it [sic] comes with the polishing sugar, body mask, and body moisture cream." Notice nothing is stated about whether the product is for women or men of a certain age or with certain skin issues. It is all about the product itself—a prime example of the me-me-me approach.

The second line of copy read: "Let's discuss the scent. All three of these products have the signature (x) scent, this gives us the same energy as the (x) lip stuff from (another company). Basically, think citrusy. This is a very strong scent. It takes getting used to." The post still hasn't told me why I would want to "get used to" the scent. How is it going to solve a problem for me? So far, all I am hearing is the me-me-me approach!

The third line of copy said, "These three are amazing. I like to use them in order. It keeps my skin feeling softer than ever, and I prefer using all three at night to wake up with smooth and soft skin." Finally I understand that these products work together and are for people who have rough skin and want smoother, softer skin. Perhaps if that was said in the first line of copy, people would be more likely to want to read on and perhaps buy the products.

The Worst First Date

For another example of the me-me-me approach, let's look at a dating situation. How much would you enjoy the first date if the other person went on and on about themself and showed no interest in learning anything about you?

What if your date never asked you a question but simply made assumptions about what you like, what you don't like, what you want out of life, and so on? For example, if your first meeting is at a restaurant for dinner, how would you feel if your date ordered for you without waiting for you to make a choice for yourself or asking about your food preferences first?

Would you feel cared for? Would you have any interest in agreeing to another date?

This example embodies how many salespeople have been taught to behave. They were taught that once you get a foot in the door, be sure to tell them how great your products and services are and why they should buy them before they have a chance to tell you no.

Unfortunately, this approach is exactly the reason why prospects say no. Your prospects don't want to hear about or talk about you. They want to talk about what is on their mind and heart, and they want to hear that you are listening to them.

We need to move on and shift from the me-me-me sales approach to the "I care about you, you, you!" Alignment Marketing Formula.

The Solution

When you're starting the sales process, begin immediately by asking your prospects how they are doing and identify any problems or challenges they are facing before sharing the benefits of your product or service.

Time Is the New Money

Richard Branson is known for saying, "Time is the new money!"[2]

Remember this important principle when you want to make sales. One of the most valuable ways we can show our prospects and customers we care is by appreciating the value of their time by not wasting it. Ask how much time they can give us and stay within that limit.

And always ask about them first before talking about yourself and what you are selling.

Satisfy Their Emotions

Another way we can give our prospects and customers value is through how we communicate with them.

Emotion plays a huge part in creating any satisfying relationship, especially in a sales situation. If prospects' needs are fulfilled, they will feel contented, excited, or joyful—and much more likely to make a purchase from you.

However, if your prospects feel their needs were unmet, they might be left feeling frustrated, hurt, or confused—and not at all likely to make a purchase from you.

David Meerman Scott agrees: "Truly understanding the market problems that your products and services solve for your buyer, you transform your marketing from mere product-specific, ego-centric gobbledygook that only you understand and care about into valuable information people are eager to consume and that they use to make the choice to do business with your organization."[3]

Help Them Succeed Quickly

Elisa Mardegan helps cut through the confusion of social media marketing for her ideal audience. Regarding her first conversations with prospects for her coaching program, she says, "I don't just tell them what they should do, I give them something to do to produce results. It shows them I care about them . . . not just there for a sale. I want them to succeed right away . . . even before they hire me."

First, be sure you know how the product or service you sell will solve any or all problems with achieving their own goals. (See chapter 5 for the 6 typical categories of personal challenges.)

Then, when in a conversation with your prospects, begin by asking questions to determine which of these problems they want to solve.

Now you know where to focus your attention to provide an emotionally satisfying experience for your prospects.

Envision Your Success

After you quickly establish their needs, you can begin to craft your vision for how you will let your ideal prospects and audience know how much you care about them.

Your vision will be based on how you want to be of service to your ideal audience and how you want to be successful as a result.

Your *vision* has everything to do with seeing yourself as being satisfied—as being the person you want to be and making a difference in solving the problems of others in the way you want to be of service.

Once you have aligned your vision with your personality, core values, and how you want to be of service, you will know what products and services are in alignment with you and the people you want to serve.

Everything else begins to fall into place, doors start to open, and obstacles melt away like butter on a scorching hot summer day.

Do You Have What Your Audience Wants?

At this stage in the Alignment Marketing strategy, you should ensure you are aligned with a company that sells products and services that help you provide the solution to the audience that has the problems you either used to have or that currently has the same interests you do!

In order to know what products are truly aligned with your vision and values, return to your answers to the list of prompts in chapters 5 and 7. As you review your answers, ask yourself, "Who do I now feel are the people or groups of people who have the pain, challenges, or problems I used to have?"

Stephanie Oden asked herself this question. She discovered that her ideal audience is women who feel overwhelmed and don't know how to get to the next level of success in their career or as an entrepreneur. She used to be someone like that until she discovered a path of success that worked for her.

The next question toward identifying whether what you sell is in alignment with your vision is, "Do I sell products or services that can help solve their pain, challenge, or problems or help them enjoy their hobbies and interests?"

Stephanie sure did. She turned her own path to success into a coaching practice. She is now known as a life and business success strategist. She also sells to her clients the network marketing products that helped her move forward on her path.

However, if your answer to the question is no, the good news is that many companies make products or provide services that would help solve the problems of people who match your ideal audience profile. And many other companies make products and provide services that could help your audience enjoy their hobbies and interests even more.

Do your research to identify what you can sell that is in alignment with you and your audience so your vision can be fulfilled.

Where Will You Meet Your Audience?

Once you are aligned with what you are selling, you're probably going to ask, "Where will I meet people who share similar interests with me?"

On social media platforms, of course!

No matter what you are selling—whether you represent your own services, a direct selling company's products, the products and services of a Fortune 500 corporation, or you are requesting donations to a nonprofit organization—you will most easily meet people who match your ideal audience profile through social media sites. While people still make cold calls, the ease of meeting people through social media has made it the preferred method.

InsideSales gathered a few relevant data points on calls:

- Sales go to the first person who makes contact with the prospect 50 percent of the time.
- Reaching a prospect now takes eight cold call attempts as compared with just over three in 2007.
- Only 2 percent of cold calls end with a sale.
- Salespeople make an average eight dials per hour and search for over six hours to set just one appointment.[4]

Let's compare these facts to a Forbes study on social media:

- More than 78.6 percent of salespeople using social media get better results than those who don't.
- Salespeople with a social media presence exceed their quota by 23 percent compared to those who don't.

- Forty percent of salespeople have closed deals through social media marketing.
- Salespeople using social media spend less than 10 percent of their time finding new prospects.[5]

Examples of Where You Can Find Your Audience

Now that you know the benefits of prospecting using social media sites rather than cold calling, here are a few examples of where you can find various audiences.

If you are someone who had or still has digestive problems that have been improved by your company's products, you are the person with the answers for taming tummy tantrums. Your prospects are people with digestive problems who want the discomfort in their tummy to go away. You can likely find them in Facebook groups or following influencers in the health and wellness niche who share their content on Facebook, Instagram, YouTube, Clubhouse, Meetup, or other social media sites.

If you are someone who learned how to get out of debt or prepare for a prosperous retirement using services your company provides, you are the person with the answers for how to make savings accounts grow. Your prospects are people who want to improve their credit scores, increase their income, or save for retirement. You can likely find them following influencers in the financial arena who share their content on Facebook, LinkedIn, YouTube, Clubhouse, Meetup, and other social media sites.

If you are someone who never knew how to dress with style and now you do because of the jewelry or clothing your company provides, you are the person who can help others look so good they turn people's heads. Your prospects are people who want to feel and be more physically attractive to others. You can likely find them following fashion and style influencers on Facebook, Instagram, Pinterest, Clubhouse, TikTok, and other social media sites.

If you are someone who had trouble attracting prospects and making sales before learning how to master social media marketing strategies with your company's training programs and tools, you are the person who can help others get more leads, sales, or engagement for their posts or become an influencer on social media. Your prospects are entrepreneurs or other salespeople who are struggling to connect with their audience on social media and need to make more sales. You will meet them following the social media marketing influencers on Facebook, LinkedIn, YouTube, and other social media sites.

If you are someone who loves talking about the joys of having grandchildren and keeping them healthy and safe using your company's products or services, you are a grandparent who has easy ways for keeping your grandchildren healthy and safe. Your prospects are other grandparents who worry and would like solutions for keeping their grandchildren safe. You will meet them in groups, primarily on Facebook or Meetup, where grandparents gather to share photos of their children and grandchildren and ask questions for support and guidance about issues in their lives.

If you are retired and have hobbies and interests you enjoy, you can meet your audience in groups on Facebook dedicated to your hobbies and interests, such as travel, skiing, knitting, gardening, or playing an instrument.

If you are beginning your fitness program and you are using your company's products or services (e.g., nutritional supplements, fitness tools, equipment) to support your physical wellness success, you are the person who is willing to share the adventures of starting a workout program to get healthier and more attractive. Your prospects are other people just starting to make improvements in their fitness who need guidance to do it the right way. You can likely find them in gyms and yoga studios. However, the fastest and easiest way will be to meet them first on social media (by following fitness influencers on Facebook,

YouTube, or Instagram) or on Meetup (by finding local groups of people who want to work out together).

If you are someone who loves animals and are raising funds to support an animal rescue organization, you are the person who is standing up for animal rights and protections. Your prospects are other people who care about animal rights and protections. They are on social media, too, hanging out in groups on Facebook or Meetup dedicated to sharing information about animal rescue and adoption operations or for pet owners of specific pet breeds, such as poodles or hairless cats.

With the help of social media sites, you can easily identify people who match you and find them once you are ready. We will explore in more detail about how to meet those people who match your audience in chapter 10.

Remember, you are the person who can solve the problems and challenges of your ideal audience because you have been where they are now. You will need to first identify the type of person or group of people you can help—otherwise, you cannot know where to find them so you can start to build a relationship with them. You also won't know what to say to them to let them know you care so they will want to get to know, like, and trust you.

The Steps to a Sale

Now that you know how easy it is to find your audience, the next step is to be prepared to greet them and start a conversation about their problem or shared interest. For example, you may join a Facebook group of people who are all looking for solutions to their digestive issues. In that group you will read posts written by people asking questions related to their digestive issues. Here are the steps you can take to get a sale:

Step 1: Know—Send people friend requests to let them know you are both members of the same group and that you care they are having digestive issues.

Step 2: Know—Let them know you have had your own experience with digestive upsets.

Step 3: Like—Offer to share your experience with them if they would like to know the solution you have found to your problem.

Step 4: Like—If they accept your offer of a conversation, you now have the opportunity to ask questions and discover more about your new friend, such as how long they have had the digestive issue, what else they have already tried to relieve it, and why it is so important to them to have this problem resolved. These types of questions demonstrate your acknowledgment of and empathy for them.

Step 5: Trust—As you ask these questions and receive the answers, you will know just how strong their commitment is to having the problem resolved. If the level of urgency and commitment is at a ten on a scale of one to ten, then offer the solution and make a sale.

Of course, not everyone you contact will accept your friend request or reply to your message. But those who are ready to hear solutions to their problem will respond to you.

Not all of those people will be ready to take action in that time. Those who are not ready can remain your friend. Ask them to share their reason for not being ready to take action to resolve their problem. You may also want to ask them about their core values at this moment to ensure they are in alignment with yours.

You may discover their reason is something you cannot resolve. Sometimes they just would like more information, which you can then provide.

Other times they want you to check back with them at a later date. If that's the case, as they say, the ball is in your court. You can choose to maintain the friendship whether or not you can resolve their problem. You can do this by providing the additional information they are requesting or checking back with them on a specific day and time to which you both agree. At this point, you can go back to the same group of other people who want to resolve digestive issues and start over again.

Meeting Prospects in Groups

In addition to those who are posting in the group, be sure to reach out and send friend requests to other people in the same group because many people do not feel comfortable writing a post. They prefer to read what other people have written. They are members of the group because they want information.

You can find them by reading the comments to posts started by other members. Be the person who reaches out first to say hi to those who comment on posts, then follow the steps above.

If you are making friends with people who are following influencers in your niche and making comments on their posts and videos, follow the same steps to a sale as outlined above.

Create a Group

The best way I have found to continue building a strong relationship with both prospects who have become friends and clients or customers is to invite them into a private group I have created where I offer a steady flow of content they would want to read and watch that addresses their challenges and problems. This content creates the satisfying emotional experience they are craving.

When they see my commitment to providing content in this group regularly, I have now become an influencer and a leader because I consistently provide wisdom and information that makes their lives better.

I encourage you to do the same. Whether on Facebook, LinkedIn, YouTube, Clubhouse, Instagram, TikTok, or another platform, be sure to create your own group (like a private club) where only your friends and fans can receive valuable content that makes their life better in the way they want.

The more consistent you are at providing valuable information and content, the faster you will gain their trust. Once trust is established, you will be the person they buy from once they are ready to buy.

Reciprocity Strengthens Trust

As trust builds, you will start to inspire reciprocity—an exchange for mutual benefit. They will start giving you a yes to what you are offering, and they will give you money for it.

In fact, when you get really good at delivering value, your audience will be reaching out to you and asking for recommendations on how to solve their problems. People will send you requests to know more about what you have to offer.

Delivering valuable content requires us to show empathy. Let's explore how empathy maintains alignment in the next chapter.

CHAPTER 9

Empathy Is Easier to Show to Our Ideal Prospects

SHOWING EMPATHY GOES AGAINST what is taught by old-school sales training programs. Showing empathy and concern is considered a handicap if you want to "win the sale." This couldn't be more wrong.

The Problem

Empathy requires vulnerability. Many people associate vulnerability with being weak. Sales training programs usually focus on how to make sales by "keeping the upper hand," "not letting your guard down," and "staying in control." These programs teach the importance of using facts and logic rather than emotion.

However, in study after study, researchers have found that the most logical argument in the world does not change people's minds until emotional elements are also addressed.

How to Know If You Are Selling Based on Logic

Have you ever heard a prospect say any of the following statements after you have made your sales offer?

- "We're very impressed and will give it some thought!"
- "What you say makes a lot of sense. Let me run it by the others."
- "We need to think about it, and I'll get back to you."

If so, you were using logic instead of empathy in your presentation.

You may have left them thinking you might be able to solve the problem but not feeling that you absolutely understood and will solve the problem. The empathy was missing.

No empathy = no sales!

The Solution

Empathy and emotion win over logic. According to Brené Brown, professor, lecturer, author, and podcast host, "Vulnerability is the core, the heart, the center of meaningful human experiences."[1]

Expanding on this point, "The truth," according to change strategist Makeda Pennycooke, "is being vulnerable requires an incredible amount of courage and courage requires strength. As Maslow demonstrated, we all have basic needs and desires. So neediness is kind of a given as a human."[2]

To further this point, 95 percent of our purchase decisions, according to Harvard Business School professor Gerald Zaltman, take place unconsciously. They take place at the level of our core values, which is why empathy plays such an important part in marketing and sales. Michael Harris, CEO of Insight Demand, writes, "Our subconscious/intuitive decision to buy is communicated to the conscious mind via an emotion. The conscious mind then searches for rational reasons, and that's how we complete the circle: We justify our emotional signals to buy with logical reasons. Phew, the illusion is now complete that the conscious mind that we identify with is in control so we can feel safe and secure."[3]

If you don't speak first to your prospects on an emotional level, you're just one more person trying to sell them something.

Be Yoda

Empathy is created by sharing how you, or someone you know, have experienced similar challenging situations and how your products or services solved the same problem. This level of empathy leads to sales.

Empathy is demonstrated through telling our personal stories, being transparent, being authentic, being human, and not acting like a two-dimensional billboard or a commercial for our products and services.

Rockson Samuel, a writer, marketer, and dentist, explained, "People are literally walking around talking to themselves about why they're in pain or why they can't get that bright future that they think they and their family deserve. They have emotions wrapped up around this. They want to feel like they can be the Luke Skywalker in their own hero's journey through their own life. Your job is to be Yoda."[4]

This is what the old saying, "People buy on emotion and justify on logic" boils down to. By your consistently creating valuable content for your prospects and even your existing clients or customers, they can continue to get to know, like, and trust you.

To be like Yoda is to be the wise one who provides the answers.

Providing Valuable Content

First you need to know that valuable content can include

- Tips for solving problems people have
- Step-by-step instructional guides to achieve something they desire
- Personal stories about your life that in some way relate to the problem they want to solve
- Anything that helps them see their problems from a more positive perspective, including customer testimonials

Of course, making this information available for free helps.

Here is how Elisa Mardegan practices this principle:

I spend time in groups on Facebook where people match my audience. I meet people there and take the conversation out of the group to explore what else we have in common. After a few written private messages back and forth, if I feel it is okay with them, then I will use the voice message feature through FB Messenger to build rapport by asking them about common interests I find on their personal profile page. I choose voice messaging so they can hear my voice and excitement, and it is almost like we are talking face to face.

I continue to explore if they are a fit for me—and if I am a fit for them—by asking them how they got into their business, how much they enjoy it, or if it is a hobby or if they want to grow it larger. I ask what struggles they have with growing their business. When they respond back to me with what is causing them the most trouble, I respond via voice message again to offer a tip to help ease the struggle. I end by saying if they want any more tips they can schedule a free consult with me via Zoom. During the consult, I make an offer of which product or service I have to sell that will solve their problems most effectively.

Make Your Content Visible to the Public

If you choose to do what Elisa does, people may do some research on you first to see whether they feel you are in alignment with them. They might check out your social media accounts and website to see what type of tips and solutions you offer to determine whether they want to use their time to connect and engage with you.

If they get at least one emotionally satisfying experience from your content, they will probably accept your friend request, wanting to build a relationship with you that will likely result in a sale.

This is why you need to make sure your posts are public and focus on topics that are of interest to your ideal audience. If your Facebook profile page or Instagram page are set to private so that only close friends and family can see your posts, give your profile a makeover!

Create a private group on Facebook or a separate Instagram account that is only for people who are close to you and who do not match your ideal audience of prospects. You can say whatever you want to say to those close friends and family. Then keep your main profile page set to public for prospects who want to get to know who you are, what you stand for, and what problems you help solve.

No matter which social media platforms you use, always remember that from now on your pages are meant to be a means for providing valuable content to people who match your ideal audience profile. Be sure to create and share only content that would be interesting for them to read. Provide tips and solutions that solve their problems.

Be in the Caring-about-People Business

Make sure your business shows you care about people and solving their problems. For example, someone who represents a dog food company could be posting dog training tips along with solutions for dealing with common canine health challenges. A life coach could share mindset and success tips. A social media expert could share marketing trends and solutions to the most common social media marketing mistakes. A representative for a company that sells paper products to businesses could offer tips and solutions for saving time, money, and resources.

You may have heard online business owners and marketers say, "The money is in your list." That's partly true. Yes, building a massive email list of customers and prospects who are aligned with us has some benefits. The real money, though, is in the relationships you have with the people on that list.

Always remember, you are in the caring-about-people business! Take the target off of people's foreheads and choose to make a caring connection, one that is emotionally satisfying so they want to say yes to you.

Below is an example of a blog post I wrote to be emotionally compelling and satisfying to an audience of people with foot and ankle problems. How many ways can you find that I let my audience know I empathize with their problems?

Until recently, my swollen ankles used to make me cry with pain. 😰

It was just something I lived with for years and knew would likely happen if I was on my feet too long. 🫤

Sometimes they would also swell just from sitting too long. 🫠

Today I am crying tears of joy...because my feet are ready to feel just as GOOD at the end of a day of holiday shopping...as they do at the beginning. 👣 🫧

NO MORE SORE TOOTSIES or SWOLLEN ANKLES for me anymore! 📣😄

And my VARICOSE VEINS are also shrinking...which is ridiculously WONDERFUL since nothing else has ever worked. 😩 💯

I wonder if my problems stem back to having to wear corrective braces on my feet as a kid. Hmmmm. 😌

My father had 'diabetic feet' and knee and back issues. Sure wish this was around to have helped him. 🖤

I am so glad I FINALLY decided I had nothing to lose. 😇 👋

Much less-expensive than everything else I have ever tried...which is such a BONUS.

And another BONUS...nothing to take internally...because I have many dietary limitations...so I love nothing to put in my tummy.

Can you hear my HAPPINESS? I feel giddy with joy.

Or shall I say...I have 'happy feet'? Because it's true and they wanted to share their joy. 😌

Not once did I mention the name of the company that makes the product that solved my problem. Yet I had an abundance of people reach out to me to ask for more information, and I sold thousands of dollars in products from this one blog post.

I did this by giving them an emotionally satisfying experience. I did not provide a list of logical reasons why they should buy my product. Instead, I shared with them my emotions about being in pain—emotions they have too. I was willing to be vulnerable, authentic, and personal. And then I shared my emotions about no longer being in pain—emotions they would love to experience too.

I receive such wonderful responses to my posts and emails because I have been consistently (daily) posting solutions to the problems of my audience. They have come to know me, like me, and trust me because they know I care about them. When I tell them about the problems and challenges I have overcome, they feel comfortable asking me how I did it. They feel in alignment with me and vice versa. They feel like they are asking a close friend because that is how I make them feel.

How to Craft a Message
That Produces Sales

If you want to write blog posts or share your message via videos that make your ideal audience feel comfortable, start with crafting one simple statement that demonstrates you know the problem you solve. Next, state you have a method or process for solving it. Finish by explaining what the prospect can expect as the solution to the problem.

For example, let's return to the skin-care product in chapter 8. Below I will now demonstrate how to write a post in a way that conveys empathy to the ideal audience for that product.

- First, I identify the problem I know I can solve: *itchy, rough, or dry skin.*

- Then, I identify the method I have for solving it: *I have a proven process to increase moisture in the skin.*
- I finish with the desired outcome or solution the ideal audience wants: *a silky, smooth, and more radiant appearance.*

To put the principle of "show how much you care first" into action, I have rewritten the copy for an Instagram post using these three elements and adding a lot of care and empathy:

First Line—Do you suffer with itchy, rough, or dry skin? Have you tried product after product and your skin still doesn't feel smooth and silky to the touch? Are you literally uncomfortable in your own skin?

Second Line—You may find it comforting to know that often the cause of these irritating skin conditions is due to a lack of moisture—and that the problem has an easy solution. The top layer of skin is made up of dead cells and natural oils, which help to capture moisture and keep the skin soft and smooth. Skin problems occur when there's not enough water in this top layer of cells.

Third Line—If you want a softer, smoother appearance, you will want to experience this three-step system of luxurious care to increase your skin's moisture. This beauty-boosting trio contains a polishing sugar, body mask, and body moisture cream.

Giving Them the Option to Self-Select

By starting this post with questions, I invited prospects to self-select according to their level of interest right away. If they stay, it is because they are aligned with what I was asking. They immediately know I have their interests in mind and heart.

Follow this communication process to demonstrate you care for your ideal audience and their problems.

Step 1: Acknowledge their problem and ask questions about how they feel about the problem.

Step 2: Explain what causes the problem.

Step 3: Provide the solution to the problem.

Do these steps no matter if you are writing a social media post or ad, creating a live video, hosting a webinar, or speaking one on one with a prospect.

This process of demonstrating care and empathy builds trust faster, which makes it possible for sales to occur faster, without being pushy, spammy, or salesy.

CHAPTER 10

Where Will You Find Your Ideal Audience— Those Who Want You to Solve Their Problems?

Consistently asking your prospects questions—either by creating content or beginning actual conversations with them—is likely to lead to more sales.

Social media content to attract people who fit your ideal audience profile can be in the form of videos, Facebook posts, blog posts, or Instagram posts or stories. Your content can also be in the form of a PDF download, how-to infographics, cheat sheets, audio clips, or interviews—anything you want to offer to show your ideal audience how much you care.

Where Would You Go to Get Answers?

Now it's time to actually find out where people who match your ideal audience profile are hanging out so you can share this content with them.

Are they more likely to be on Facebook, Instagram, YouTube, Twitter, LinkedIn, Pinterest, Clubhouse, watching TED Talks, or reading the blogs of influencers?

You might say to me, "Stacey, I don't know where they are."

And I will respond, "Yes, you do!"

Where Would You Go to Get Answers?

Your ideal audience is just like you. When you were looking for answers, where did you go to find them? If you were still in pain, where would you go online to get ideas for solutions? If you still had digestive issues, where would you go online to get ideas of how to tame your tummy? If you still had bad credit, where would you go online to get ideas for how to get out of debt? If you are a knitter, where do you go online to get knitting tips? If you are a grandparent, where do you go online to talk with other grandparents? If you want fashion tips, where would you go online to get style ideas? If you want information about ways to cut costs and expenses in your business, where would you go to get suggestions?

It's just that simple.

Maybe you would watch TikTok or YouTube videos. Or maybe you would join a Facebook or LinkedIn group. Or maybe you would scroll through Instagram or Pinterest or join a Clubhouse club.

Where you would go is where your ideal audience is also likely to go. As you saw from the various examples I provided in chapter 8, you can easily find people who match your ideal audience profile on social media sites.

Don't Spread Yourself Too Thin

One mistake that many salespeople make is they attempt to make friends across numerous sites at the same time. Most marketers just spam their links everywhere, provide no value to their prospects, solve no problems, and then wonder why nobody is buying what they are selling. That's like trying to attend five different networking meetings spread out across town in the space of two hours in order to meet as many different people as possible as fast as possible.

That approach is fine if all you want to do is hand out business cards and hope that someone you met briefly will call you and ask for more information. That approach does not work if you want people to know, like, and trust you.

As explained previously, it takes a bit of conversation to determine if someone is a match to your ideal audience profile. We have also explored how consistency shortens the time it takes to build up trust, which is required for making a sale. Because of this, choose only one platform first and become known for hanging out there. Be a familiar face to the others in the group or those following the same influencer. As they see you participating where they are comfortable spending their time, they will feel comfortable with you. They will consider you to be inside their comfort zone, and you will have shortened the length of time required to build trust and make an offer leading to a sale.

Once you have established yourself on one platform, then you can begin to slowly expand to other platforms, but only if your audience hangs out there too.

Remember your goals:

Build your audience—As you meet people who match your ideal audience profile, you can send them friend requests and messages to build a relationship with each one. This is how they come to know you.

Engage your audience—As they read your posts and watch your videos that focus on providing the solutions to their problems, they will begin to respond to your messages. This is how they get to like you and become comfortable with you.

Sell to your audience—As they build trust in you, they will say yes to what you offer.

And bingo! You are now reaping the benefits of Alignment Marketing.

In chapter 11, I am going to show you how to ditch the spammy sales script and what to say in your posts, video messages, and one-to-one conversations that will build trust much faster so you can make your sales offer faster.

PART 4

Are You in Alignment with What You Are Saying?

MOST SALESPEOPLE HAVE BEEN TAUGHT that the most valuable weapon in their arsenal is their script. Sales trainers will tell you it is your best defense against the objections your audience is sure to express as the reasons they cannot or will not buy from you. They will tell you to memorize your script to be armed and ready to fight back.

In this section, I will explain all the reasons to ditch the script. I will also share how the script itself is one of the major reasons why people do not buy.

As you now know from reading part 3, our prospects must experience an emotionally satisfying experience with us for them to feel they can trust us and then buy from us. Scripts tend to focus on the logical benefits of the product or service and keep you locked in your mind and locked out of your emotions as well as your prospects'.

I love this quote from *Entrepreneur* magazine: "Using a sales script is a conventional way for a business to scale a branded sales approach. It may allow a business to execute a sale with those who don't notice or don't care that it's using a script. Ultimately, however, sales scripts will time and time again fall short of creating a personal and emotional connection."[1]

Carla Archer found this to be true when representing a company that required her to use the same script with every prospect.

In this section I will provide you with suggestions of questions to ask your prospects to make it easy to personalize conversations with each of them and that become emotionally comfortable and satisfying to you both.

I will be supporting you in shifting from someone who relies on scripts to someone who is an empathetic problem solver.

CHAPTER 11

Ditch the Script!

MOST SALESPEOPLE LEARN THE SCRIPTS their company provides. They repeat those scripts as if they are robots spitting out facts without emotion. They are discouraged from adding anything personal into the script to ensure that all the information is conveyed exactly as the company wants it to be conveyed. Basically they are hired to be a walking billboard.

The Problem

Most people do not grow up wanting to be a walking billboard. And for this reason, sales positions remain one of the top three most difficult jobs to fill.

Scripts as Weapons

Another reason for teaching salespeople to speak from scripts is to ensure they are prepared to deal with objections. As Sam Horn said, "Scripts control the conversation." Scripts teach salespeople to prepare to control. They are taught to anticipate that the conversation will end in the sales offer being rejected. As soon as salespeople hear an objection come out of the prospect's mouth, they have a ready-made answer to deal with it. The terminology is to "strike it down."

Renowned sales consultant Ian Altman wrote, "A major mistake is that the salesperson is reading the script, but not paying attention to the answers."[1] By not paying attention to the answers, salespeople are not truly acknowledging the person who is their prospect. They are simply listening for the objections to pop up. And lack of acknowledgment, as we have explored in detail previously, means a missed opportunity to find alignment and make a deeper connection.

While salespeople armed with a script (notice the word *armed*) are prepared to talk with the prospect, they listen to the prospect only to be ready to counterattack the objection (notice the word *counterattack* too).

Salespeople trained in this way do not know how to truly listen, show empathy, explore where they are aligned with the prospect, or focus on building trust first before offering something for sale.

Without alignment, there is no engagement. Without engagement there is no trust building. Without trust, there are no sales.

The Solution

Ditch the script and become someone known as an authentically empathetic problem solver. Remember, you are the brand that your audience wants—not the company and not the products.

Thierry Alexandre found the solution. He connects with people on an authentic level. He starts a relationship by being curious about what is going on in their lives. He looks at their social media profiles before contacting them to learn what is important to them. Have there been any births, deaths, or parties in their world? What quotes have they shared? When he starts the conversation, he asks them questions related to those topics.

According to an article in *Entrepreneur* magazine, "Consumer research from Stackla reveals that while 86 percent of consumers report that authenticity is an important factor for which brands they support, 57 percent feel that fewer than half of companies create truly authentic content. To ensure your storytelling is truly authentic, all branding efforts should ultimately grow from your values and goals. This will attract like-minded customers who view supporting your brand as a reflection of their values."[2]

Make People Feel Something

Writing for AdAge, Matthew Luhn, a writer at Pixar and best-selling author of *The Best Story Wins*, states, "The goal of advertising is not to convince people or make them think something. It's to make them *feel* something."[3] This is true of ads, Facebook posts, YouTube videos, and one-to-one conversations with a prospect or client.

Authenticity is important when telling stories. Luhn continues, "Stories are the best way to connect on an emotional level with people. For that to happen, you need to use personal and shared experiences to connect with a specific audience. . . . All good story plots are based on desires thwarted, scary situations, people trying to accomplish something, failing, and then eventually succeeding."

We all have lived through these types of stories and survived to tell them, which is why I invited you to answer questions in chapter 5. If you answered those questions, you now know the major problems over which you have triumphed. The next step is to craft your experiences into authentic stories that show your ideal audience you understand the problems they are experiencing and have the solution to those problems.

Here are a few suggestions of the problems you and they might encounter through life:

- Experiencing pain (physical, emotional, or both)
- Feeling unattractive in some way
- Being buried under a pile of debt
- Feeling unappreciated
- Feeling awkward while learning to play a sport or a musical instrument
- Putting one's own needs aside to be a caregiver of someone else—children or other loved ones
- Feeling trapped in a dead-end job

I am sure you can add dozens, if not hundreds, of other problems and challenges you and others have encountered as you have lived your life.

Choose One

For now, just choose one problem you no longer have that you can help someone else overcome by using your products or services. Or choose one hobby you and many others enjoy and consider how using your products or services makes it possible to enjoy that hobby even more. Does your product or service help them have more time to give to the hobby? Does your product or service make them feel better in some way so they can spend more time doing the hobby?

One Major Problem Produces Other Problems

Often, one of these large problems produces other problems. For instance, let's look at the situation of people buried under a pile of debt. Because they have so much debt, they may also

- Experience emotional stress because of worrying about the bills

- Work long hours and not take time for good self-care, so they start to become ill
- Feel embarrassed because they are not successful the way they want to be, which is having a negative effect on their personal and business relationships
- Not feel safe or happy about where they are living, but it's all they can afford
- Not have the relationship with their children that they want if they only had more time and money and energy

If you have been in this person's shoes yourself and you triumphed over these problems, you have many authentic stories to tell in your posts, blog articles, video messages, and one-to-one conversations. You are a credible authority to the person who is still dealing with the problem. You can easily and honestly show empathy to the members of your ideal audience.

Tell Your Story Consistently

You will next need to identify how the products or services you sell can help this person. Even if you were not using these products and services at the time you solved the problem for yourself, you can now imagine how your products or services could have helped you in some way. That personal story is what you will want to tell consistently in all your communications to attract your ideal audience and begin an aligned relationship that leads to sales.

A reminder that this is how the Alignment Marketing Formula works:

$$\text{Alignment} + \text{Belief} \times \text{Consistency} = \text{Sales, Satisfaction, and Success}$$

As long as you (1) authentically believe your core values are aligned with your products or services, (2) can serve others who have the problems you used to have or want to learn how to do something you learned how to do, and (3) consistently share your story with people who fit your ideal audience profile, you can expect to make sales while experiencing greater satisfaction and success.

Here are the steps to telling your authentic story in an emotionally satisfying way to your audience.

Step 1—Identify the main problem of your ideal audience (which is, of course, one of the problems you used to have). For example, let's say your ideal audience is human resources (HR) managers.

Main problem: Most HR managers feel they have so many responsibilities and not enough time to do them well.

Solution: Whatever you want to sell them, be sure that you can help them manage more in less time (be more productive).

Step 2—Identify the subproblems your ideal audience also has because of the main problem. For example, here are some possible subproblems for HR managers:

- Attracting and retaining the right people for each position in the company
- Helping the company staff to deal with change that occurs frequently
- Developing leaders from within the company
- Providing education and other support resources to all company staff
- Managing diversity requirements
- Ensuring health and safety requirements are met
- Maintaining employee satisfaction
- Feeling like a babysitter most of the time

Step 3—Whether you choose to attract prospects who are HR managers by writing social media posts or blog articles, sharing your message via video, sending an email, or making a cold call, make sure you are sharing how you personally resolved—or are in the process of resolving—at least one of these problems. If you do, the likelihood of scheduling a face-to-face meeting is much higher than if you don't.

Let your prospects know you used to feel, be, or suffer the way they are now and you can feel their pain because you have been where they are now. Affirm that you understand they have all of this on their plate and more. They want to hear you care about what they are going through by identifying the problems and offering solutions.

In the case of HR managers, they may also enjoy hearing how other HR managers are handling the same issues, problems, and challenges. In addition to sharing your personal stories, you could also share how you have solved problems for others in their position. For example, you can ask yourself, "When HR managers have a complaint or a frustration, who can they go to get it off their chest?" In this way, you can be helpful in connecting them with other HR managers you know.

You could even start a networking or support group for HR managers and hear firsthand their problems and issues so you can then address and help resolve them. Although they may belong to professional associations, their participation is paid for by the company that employs them. They must present a professional face at association meetings because they are representing their company.

On the other hand, if you were to organize a let-your-hair-down, after-hours gathering of friends who just happen to hold similar positions, you will likely find that the professional face gets dropped and honest feelings and real information are shared. This is where true friendships are forged.

If you are the one to make introductions to other people in similar positions or create a networking group and invite those in similar positions to attend, you have now become the trusted authority to your ideal audience. You are now the one who stands out among all the salespeople serving HR managers.

Because you thought about how to help them in a way that goes beyond just selling a product or service, you have become aligned with your prospects in another way that is satisfying to them. And you are likely to get the sale over and over again from each of these HR managers.

What They Think about You

By continuously identifying ways to help them solve the problems they face, you can expect to become an important part of their life. They will think the following about you if you consistently offer valuable solutions to their problems in all your communications:

- They understand my pain.
- Yes, I will continue to follow them.
- Yes, I will continue to read/watch/listen to them.
- Yes, I will buy their products and services because they obviously care about helping me to be successful the way I want to be.

CHAPTER 12

How to Close More Sales and Build More Profitable Relationships

IF YOU WANT TO CLOSE a sale, don't be in a hurry to make the offer before trust has been built.

The Problem

Most people in sales start selling (or pitching) as the first step, hoping to get the person to respond and then hoping to eventually build a long-term relationship with the prospect.

That is what Stephanie Oden was taught to do too. She said the sales training she received was focused on convincing her that she was supposed to make an offer to everyone with a pulse—whether she knew them or not or they were interested or not. Based on her core values, she did not feel comfortable with that approach.

Doing sales this way is what gets good people labeled as pushy and spammy. Don't sell yourself out by selling to your prospects too early.

Most salespeople have at one point rushed into closing a sale prematurely. The reasons typically stem from one of the following:

- The sales manager told them what to do and when to do it.
- They were trying to make their monthly quota and time was running out.
- They misjudged the prospect's intentions by not asking enough questions.

Nick Kane of the Janek Performance Group wrote, "Turning a sale into a rush job is a little like giving a canned sales presentation that includes a list of impressive features, but that never really deep dives into how your product and/or service will work as a great fix for the customer's dilemma."[1]

His words reinforce what I explained in chapter 6—we must take our time moving through the Know, Like, and Trust process of building an aligned relationship.

The Solution

You must build and engage before you can sell anything.

To avoid rushing in too fast, you must know for certain where you and your prospects are aligned. You must also be certain you can solve their problem with your product or service.

You must know what problems they are facing that they do not know how to solve. You must be able to convey with authentic empathy that you understand their problems because you have also experienced the same challenges. And you must believe that you have the products or services that are the best solutions to those problems.

When you consistently engage with your prospects with empathy, they will feel your belief, and their trust in you will grow. They feel you have their best interests at heart. They feel comfortable with you because you feel authentically and passionately in alignment with yourself and what you are offering. When they feel they can trust in you, they will say yes to what you have to offer.

There is no need for scripts to overcome objections. You will not hear an objection at this point. You do not need to put on your battle armor because there is no war. You have no need for a product-focused script. You can both stay in your personal comfort zones, where they will make a purchase from you.

Are you now wondering how to consistently engage without being pushy and spammy? You will want to begin your conversation with a prospect by asking them questions rather than assuming you know the answers.

The types of questions will depend on whether you are selling to another business or directly to the consumer:

- Business-to-business sales: You sell products and services that are paid for by a company, and the person who is the decision maker is an employee of the company.
- Business-to-consumer sales: You sell products and services that are paid for personally by the people who will actually use the product or service themselves or for a family member.

In either situation, do your best to avoid the me-me-me approach of sharing your experience and the benefits of your products or services before you have asked your prospects about themselves.

It's simple to know what questions to ask when you have answered the questions for yourself in chapter 5. Those questions will help you discover what problems you have experienced, how you solved them, and how your products and services are the solution to help other people with the same problem too.

Below are two examples of how to share the knowledge of the problems and the products in different types of prospecting situations.

Business-to-Business Selling

My prospect in this example is a human resources manager. I am selling a corporate wellness program to her company.

I am having my first person-to-person conversation with this sales prospect. We are talking via Zoom after meeting on social media.

I begin by asking the following questions:

- Why did you want to be a human resources manager?
- What do you feel is the most rewarding part of your job?
- What do you feel is the most challenging part of your job?
- How do you deal with that challenge?

Notice I ask questions that open with "Why did you," "What do you," or "How do you" to receive full answers rather than just a yes or no. These questions help me understand my prospect's reason for being in the job, how much she enjoys it, where she feels she may be struggling, and if she has attempted to resolve the problem already. I will also be able to hear who else may be involved in the decision-making process.

I will then ask these two important questions:

- How are the wellness needs of the company's employees managed by the company?
- On a scale of one to ten, with ten being "There is no need for improvement or expansion" and one being "The entire program must be thrown out so we can start all over again," what score do you give to the state of your company's wellness program?

I offered a simple numerical rating scale, which is a great way to arrive at an objective answer quickly. You can easily measure someone's level of interest about what you are asking this way.

If she answers with a ten, I ask her to tell me why her program works so well and why it does not need improvement. As I listen to the reasons, I may discover the situation is not really perfect after all and that some areas may need improvement.

If the score is nine or less, then I know there is room for improvement, which is an opportunity for me to help solve her problem by offering my corporate wellness program as the solution.

Once the prospect has finished her explanation and description of what can be improved, I would ask:

- Again, on a scale of one to ten, with ten being "The improvement must be made right away" and one being "The improvement is not a priority and won't be for quite a while," what score do you give to the need for this improvement?

I follow up by asking her why she assigned that score. Even if the score is a one, I will still ask this next question:

- Did you know that I have experience in helping other HR managers resolve that same problem? Would you like me to share with you what I suggested to them that fixed the problem?

If I have not personally dealt with that problem but someone else in my company has experience in this area, I will ask this:

- Did you know I work with someone who has experience in helping other HR managers resolve that same problem? Would you like me to share with you what they suggested would solve the problem?

If my prospect has any interest at all in solving this problem, she is likely to say yes. This then opens the door for me to tell my story or what I know of my fellow employee's story of the problem and how the corporate wellness program I sell solved the problem.

Once I have told my story, I end with another question:

- What was of interest to you about what I just shared with you?

Notice I am asking what she focused on during my story. If she feels there is an urgency to getting to the same solution, she will start asking me questions about timing, cost, and other details. At this point she is ready for me to make the offer. She is literally asking me to tell her.

If she does not feel any urgency to getting to the same solution, she won't ask me any questions and I know she is not ready for me to make the offer. At this point, I ask this question:

- If I could, what problem would you want me to solve for you as quickly as possible?

I understand I may not be able to solve the problem my prospect needs to have solved. I am not promising I can solve it. Instead I am offering an ear to listen and the possibility that I may know someone or have a suggestion that can help her. I am simply showing concern and empathy for what is of most importance to this person.

Most importantly, I want this person to remember me as someone who cared about her even if I did not make a sale that day.

As the saying goes, "People don't care how much we know. They only want to know how much we care about them."

Business-to-Consumer Selling

As another example, let's say I'm selling weight loss products direct to consumers. I am meeting someone who matches my ideal audience profile in a group on Facebook where weight loss tips are being offered and exchanged. I send out a friend request and have a conversation via messages to get to know my prospect by discovering our mutual interests in addition to weight loss.

I begin the transition to the sales offer by asking him these questions:

- Since we are both members of [name of group], what's the best weight loss tip you have received from someone in the group?
- What results did you get?

In comparison to a business-to-business conversation, when we speak to people about their personal lives, we want to go slower and ask more general questions at the beginning of getting to know them.

His answers to these questions about our common group tell me how active he is in the group and how satisfied he is with the information shared in the group. It also lets me know how well he followed the instructions and the strength of his commitment to lose weight.

He will likely ask about the best weight loss tip I have received from the group. I respond authentically:

- I am enjoying celebrating other people's results. I haven't tried any tips yet because what I am doing is working so well for me. I have lost [x] pounds and I am now maintaining my ideal weight.

I don't say anything more about what I am doing. If he is interested at that point, he will ask me. Instead, I ask him this question:

- What is your goal date? I would like to cheer you on.

Most people will not have set a goal date or they are sure they will not achieve their goal by their planned end date.

At this point, I respond with my own authentic story, such as this:

- You may not know that I was in the same situation [x number of years or months] ago. I also did not feel I would be successful at dropping the weight by a certain date. I had tried so many different programs and none of them helped me keep the weight off. I felt disappointed and frustrated with myself. And I was embarrassed by my appearance. Does this make sense?

Along with telling him my authentic story, I'm also asking him if he feels or has felt the same way as I just described.

If he says no to the question, I know immediately he will not likely say yes to an offer of weight loss products because he is not aligned with the problems I described. If this happens, I would wish him all the best and move on to making more friendships with other people in the group.

If he does say yes to the question "Does this make sense?" I can then ask:

- Why does this make sense to you?

As I listen to his answer, I can find out if he feels the same way I did. And if he does, then I ask:

- Would you like to know what I did that changed everything for me in a positive way and has helped me reach my goal and keep the weight off?

He is likely to say yes.

Next I could ask this:

- On a scale of one to ten, with ten being "I can't wait to hear more" and one being "I am just being polite," where are you on the scale right now?

If his answer is eight or less, I tell him this:

- Okay, I understand that this is not a priority for you at this time. Is there any other way you would like support?

If his answer is nine or ten, I say this:

- Okay, it will be easier for me to tell you by phone or Zoom. Do you have five minutes now?

If he says now is not a good time, I let him know I am available at one other time today and one other time tomorrow and ask which one is better for him. If those times don't work and he is truly interested, he will ask for another time option that would work.

When we meet, I keep the conversation brief since I asked for only five minutes. I start by reminding him that I am having the conversation so I can share what I did that worked for me to lose weight and keep it off. I share the following points within the first five minutes of conversation:

- Why I wanted to lose the weight
- How frustrated I was before I found the products I now sell
- How I found the products I now sell
- How fast the products made a positive difference for me
- How my life has changed in a positive way as a result of using these products

One sentence explanations for each of the above is all that is required. I keep it simple so he can easily understand how the problem was solved by the products I sell.

I then ask this question:

- On a scale of one to ten, with ten being "I want those same results as fast as possible" and one being "Thank you and I am not interested in having those results," where are you on the scale?

If his answer is an eight or less, it means the problem I am solving is not a priority to address at this time. I could respond with this:

- Okay, I understand that this is not a priority for you at this time. Is there any other way you would like support or could use a friend?

If his answer is again a nine or a ten, then he is letting me know he wants to resolve the problem quickly. Because I have now built up enough trust to make the product offer, I can say this:

- Great! Do you still have a few minutes so I can show you how to buy the products and help you get started?

If he says yes, I ask if he is ready to make a purchase now. He may ask me to wait while he gets his credit card. He is definitely ready to buy.

This is why I prefer to be on a video-sharing app like Zoom so I can share my screen and show him how to access the website and how to set up his own account.

I don't proceed if he responds that he wants to know how to purchase but has to get permission from a spouse or wait until payday. I will set another appointment with him on a day and time that gives him time to talk with his spouse or after he has been paid.

Now you can understand how ditching a product-focused script and asking genuinely caring questions will make it possible to personalize a conversation so both you and your prospect feel comfortable and emotionally satisfied, which will lead to closing more sales and building stronger, long-lasting, and more profitable relationships.

Follow the simple Alignment Marketing Formula, and you will ultimately arrive at the satisfying destination where your ideal prospects say yes to you.

PART 5

Daily Methods of Making Sales from within Your Comfort Zone

IF YOU FOLLOW THE Alignment Marketing Formula of Alignment + Belief × Consistency, the outcome will be sales, satisfaction, and success.

In the previous sections, I focused on the four areas of alignment and belief in yourself. In this section I offer five simple and comfortable mindset and revenue-producing methods to accomplish daily that will activate the Alignment Marketing Formula and produce results.

The key element is consistency—taking consistent action toward your sales goals. Momentum leads to money.

For many of my clients, being consistent requires a gentle and slow expansion of their comfort zone at the beginning. To expand the circumference of their zone often requires training in prioritizing, planning, and busting through mindset blocks that can interfere with taking action inspired and directed by being in alignment with their core values.

That is why in this section you will be able to play with, explore, and discover what I like to call *Comfort Zone Expanders*, which include the following:

- The top-earner secret to consistently be in motion toward your sales goals
- Methods of scheduling your day to consistently stay in alignment and experience success and prosperity
- The best way to consistently avoid comparison with others while you grow your business
- Tips on how to consistently bounce back quickly from setbacks
- A variety of ways to consistently say yes to you and celebrate every step you take up the ladder of success

When practiced daily, these five comfortable mindset and revenue-producing methods of staying consistently motivated will support you in avoiding burnout, increasing your enthusiasm, and boosting your confidence. I've introduced each method with an inspirational quote from a great thinker, past or present, to show how important and timeless these practices are. And ultimately, you will discover a deep sense of satisfaction—a powerful energy generator to stay in action and achieve sales and success!

CHAPTER 13

Self-Accountability

It is not only what we do, but also what we
do not do, for which we are accountable.
—Molière

IT TAKES COURAGE TO BE SELF-ACCOUNTABLE. It requires letting go of making others responsible for our choices. It means being responsible to ourselves for ensuring our choices are in alignment with our core values.

Every day—all throughout the day—we must summon up the courage to be self-accountable for what we choose to do and what we choose not to do.

Being Courageous

Since one of Elisa Mardegan's core values is courage, I asked her to share how she ensures that she practices self-accountability. She said, "Because one of my other core values is family, I count on myself to create a family atmosphere for my prospects and clients who join my private group." She chooses daily activities such as sharing tips in the group or sending private messages, which are comfortable for her to do, to ensure she is keeping her word to create that family feeling.

After I introduce the principle of self-accountability to my clients, they often feel being accountable and responsible is a heavy burden and uninspiring. These words convey *should* and *duty* and bring them back to being responsible to their elementary school teacher for doing their homework on time, to their father and mother for doing their chores by when they said they would do them, or any other expectations put upon them that felt like weighty burdens.

As such, it's understandable that most of us can't wait to unburden ourselves of the shoulds and have-tos with which accountability and responsibility are associated from this perspective.

Yet, from a different perspective, self-accountability has great energy and personal power inherent within it.

Self-Accountability Is the Source of Consistency

Thierry Alexandre feels self-accountability is the discipline we have over ourselves. It includes choosing to do what we told ourselves we want to do—even after the original motivation to do it is gone. In fact, his life partner knows that when Thierry says he is going to do anything, it will get done. That is because Thierry's relationship to self-accountability is strong.

How do you feel when asked, "In what ways do you choose to be able to count on yourself?" When I hear this question, it brings me back to my core values and being in alignment with myself.

Self-accountability gives us all the ability to choose which company, products, or services to represent, which problems we will help solve for others, and who we want to serve. Most importantly, it gives us the ability to powerfully choose the goals we want to achieve daily, weekly, monthly, annually, and ultimately.

All these choices must be in alignment with each other or we will get bent out of shape as we attempt to manage our day—and every day of our lives.

The Ability to Respond in Alignment

Throughout each day, I can choose how to respond to any situation or opportunity using my power of self-accountability. In fact, when partnered with self-accountability, I see *responsibility* simply as the ability to choose to respond or not to whatever shows up during my day.

Carolina M. Billings describes personal accountability as being transparent in all her dealings. She says, "I think about what it would be like to have a camera watching me all the time. It's what I do when no one is around. It's about doing the right thing when nobody is watching."

Here is how I utilize self-accountability and responsibility to stay in alignment throughout each day:

Step 1—I make a list of all the activities I *choose* to accomplish for the day. I take into account those activities I do for my self-care and my family care and those that I do to produce an income through making sales.

Step 2—I schedule time for each of these activities on my calendar with specific start and end times. (More about this in the next chapter.) I *choose* to be self-accountable for accomplishing these activities at the time I had set on my calendar. When life brings an opportunity or a situation into my day that I did not expect, I choose how I will respond—will I reschedule a previously planned activity or keep it—based on my most important self-accountability: staying in alignment with my core values.

Managing Work and Life Responsibilities

One of my core values is to provide a caring, safe, and loving home for my two dogs. I used to have a dog named Maggie, who was a beautiful and happy German shorthaired pointer. I chose to be self-accountable to schedule time daily to feeding, walking, and spending time with Maggie. At the times I set for these activities, I *responded* by actually doing the activities I had scheduled.

Another of my core values is to contribute a certain amount of income to the savings account I share with my husband, Bill. And I value attracting that income through sales of my consulting services. I chose to be self-accountable to schedule time daily to revenue-producing activities related to my consulting business. At the times I set for these activities, I responded by actually doing the activities I had scheduled.

One night, without warning, Maggie began having seizures. These events began on a Friday night with just one quick seizure, which appeared as if she were having a bad dream since it happened while she was sleeping. Acting from my self-accountability to care for Maggie, I *responded* by waking her up, comforting her until she fell back to sleep, and staying awake the rest of the night to ensure she was okay. She appeared to be just fine and I *chose not* to take her to the vet so I could keep to my schedule of revenue-producing activities.

That evening, I made sure she was sleeping peacefully before I went to sleep. In the middle of the night, my husband and I were both awakened by the sound of her metal cage banging against the floor. Maggie was experiencing another seizure, and this one was much more violent than the one the night before. We had no doubt that her care would require a trip to the vet the next day.

I *chose* to be self-accountable to my core values and responded by rescheduling my clients in order to take Maggie to the animal clinic. I chose to stay in my comfort zone where my priorities were in alignment, which gave me power to take action.

My clients understood because their core values are aligned with mine. They, too, have animal care and protection as one of their core values. Everything turned out well because I began with choosing to be self-accountable.

I Said, "No Way!"

A few years ago, a company I represented at the time released a new food product. It contained ingredients that I choose not to eat because I am allergic to them. You could say I chose to be self-accountable to maintain my health by not eating foods with ingredients my body cannot digest well.

I also chose to be self-accountable for not selling that product because I did not have my own personal story of how that item solved a problem for me. And I did not know anyone at the time that also felt it solved a problem for them.

To stay authentically true to my core value of integrity, I focused on selling other products from the company's line that I did feel were authentically in alignment with my values.

You could say I was fortunate that I was an independent representative and I could pick and choose what to sell. If I had been working for a corporation as an employee, I would not have had the freedom to decide what I would sell or not.

As I have said from the start of this book, if you cannot authentically align yourself with the products or services you are selling—if you are not comfortable representing them—then why are you selling them?

Options Are Plentiful

Thousands of companies have thousands of products and services to sell. All these companies would love to hire people who are aligned with their core values and believe in their products or services. Options are plentiful, which is why self-accountability is at the core of every choice (our responses or nonresponses) each of us makes throughout each and every day.

The only way to be strong and confident in your self-accountability is to return to chapter 3 and review your list of core values to ensure it is complete and each one inspires you.

If there are any on the list you added previously because you thought they should be there—decide now whether you *choose* for them to be there. Otherwise you can *choose* to remove them from the list.

CHAPTER 14

Scheduling for Success

Planning is a process of choosing among those many options. If we do not choose to plan, then we choose to have others plan for us.
—Richard I. Winwood

I SCHEDULE FOR SUCCESS BY CHOOSING what I will accomplish each day based on being self-accountable to my core values and goals. *By planning each day like this, I ensure I am in alignment with myself and staying within my comfort zone to keep moving forward and making sales.*

Keeping an Agreements Book

Among the thousands of clients I have served over the years, the vast majority had never experienced scheduling their days for success prior to meeting me. They rarely used an appointment book.

I like to call my appointment book an "agreements book" because it contains all the agreements I have with myself according to day and time throughout each day. It may look like an appointment book at first glance, but how I schedule for success is based on the priorities in my life.

Most people fill their mind to the brim with what they intend to get done that day, what they didn't get done the previous day, and what they want to get done tomorrow. As such, they feel overwhelmed because everything seems equally important and urgent to get done. They have no idea of what to do first and can feel they are failing at everything. With such a lack of clarity and confidence, is it any wonder they are not able to be consistent with the activities that lead to sales, satisfaction, and success?

What they are actually doing is selling out on themselves.

Stephanie Oden described it similarly when I asked her if she was comfortable with scheduling for success daily. She replied,

> Scheduling for success is requiring me to choose to expand my comfort zone. I had not taken it seriously in the past. I would often be in turmoil. I work a full-time job, build my coaching practice on the side, and represent a network marketing company as well as an affiliate marketing company. I was never sure when to schedule an appointment or not. Once I learned your concept of scheduling according to my priorities, I discovered that I had not identified my priorities and that is why I did not know what to do first, then second, and so on. I now know based on my core values, I owe it to myself to make commitments according to what is most important to me and then to keep my commitments to myself. I have an agreements book now. And I use it.

Take Smaller Bites

Have you heard the joke about how to eat an elephant?

The punch line is, "One bite at a time!"

We are meant to manage our activities in the same way—one small bite at a time.

A long time ago, my mind was so jam-packed with thoughts and wishes and dreams and daily tasks that it felt like a jumbled mess. I was choking on my thoughts. Unable to digest even one idea fully, I became exhausted with the effort, so nothing got done and I felt like a failure. What changed for me was hearing the joke about the elephant. I had been attempting to digest all my goals and activities as one big bite. I thought I had to because I had once heard, and took literally, the phrase that it was important to take "a big bite out of life."

After hearing the joke, though, I realized that a bite is a bite, not the entire elephant!

A goal appears as large as an elephant when it is first created. It takes up all the space in our mind, and then some. A goal is the proverbial pink elephant in the room.

Attempting to manage the whole goal at the same time was overwhelming and all-consuming. Finally, I made the choice to stop trying. Instead, I took the time to make a list of each and every activity (or bite) that would be required to achieve my goals. I then put them in order of priority to ensure the most important ones to accomplish received the most attention.

For example, if one of my priority goals is to create my website, I would write down the many steps toward the fulfillment of that goal: researching designs, hiring a designer, writing copy, selecting photos, and so on. If one of my goals is to grow my email list, I would write out the many steps toward the fulfillment of that goal: attracting people who meet my ideal audience profile, creating a funnel through which they would enter their email, writing content for the emails, and so on.

As I identify each of the steps, I can more easily focus on only the one step that must be accomplished before the others. This is how to take smaller bites that are easier for my mind to digest. I can also quickly ensure each activity was in alignment with my core values.

How to Schedule for Success

Thierry Alexandre schedules for success too. He says, "I keep an agreements book and on Sundays I plan my activities for the week to come based on my priorities list. Because life is unpredictable, I always give myself a free day with no activities planned so I can catch up on anything that is required."

One of my clients, Brenda Wiener, a business owner, shares her experience: "There were activities I would want to accomplish each week and never complete. As I was choosing to be more and more personally accountable to myself for completing what I had scheduled each week, this wasn't sitting very well with me. In fact, it was downright embarrassing!"

Do Not Take On Unnecessary Shoulds

Do you also find yourself moving the same activity from one week to the next over and over again because you don't ever accomplish it? It could be because the activity is not in alignment with your core values. You could be taking on unnecessary shoulds to do it. Take a moment to consider whether this is true for you.

Carolina M. Billings admits that she is working on expanding her comfort zone to schedule for success:

> I thrive on change and handling multiple things at the same time. Putting things sequentially and in a predetermined order is counterintuitive for me. Because self-accountability is another one of my core values, I choose to keep an eye on what I know must get accomplished to achieve my goal and create a life I enjoy.
>
> I schedule according to my way. I give myself flexibility of when activities get done and how. And to make scheduling even

more comfortable, I schedule time for fun, to have the quality of life I want to feel fulfilled.

Not Ever

George Campbell and Jim Packard, in their best-selling book *The Consistency Chain for Network Marketers*, suggest we consider what is in alignment with our values and what is not:

> When you are tempted to defer action, do this: Instead of saying, "I'll do it tomorrow," say "I am never going to do that. Never."
> I am never going to build a business.
> I am never going to be healthy.
> I am never going to be more knowledgeable.
> Are you comfortable with those statements? Maybe they are a little harsh. A little fatalistic. Here's what else they are. They are honest.[1]

If you honestly feel you have no desire to do something on your list, you can respond by choosing not to do it. Explore what activities would be in alignment with your core values instead.

Scheduling Freedom

For some people, scheduling for success may feel limiting and constricting. Since Elisa Mardegan's top core value is freedom, I asked her how she feels about scheduling her time in advance. She replied, "Scheduling for success actually helps me experience freedom by ensuring I do not overextend myself. I block out time that I call 'white space' to do what I want to do when I want to do it. For example, I want to be sure to have time with my kids for a half hour each day when they get home from school so I can hear about their day. I schedule for success to be sure I have that time. I love it. That said, my fifteen-year-old son probably hates it."

Prioritize and Delegate

Any activities you do want to accomplish yourself will now be scheduled on a calendar or in an appointment book in order of priority. That way, you will avoid overscheduling or overwhelming yourself.

What is the first activity (the first small bite) you want to accomplish today that will move you closer toward the achievement of your goal? Will it be a phone call, a meeting, doing research, writing a post or an email, or doing something else? What amount of time will you devote to the activity?

Once you have accomplished that activity, what's the next activity you will do to move even closer toward the achievement of your goal?

After you have accomplished the second activity, what will be your third intentional activity, and what will be your fourth, fifth, and so on? That's the most attractive way to achieve our goals—one activity at a time until the goal is fulfilled.

If you have activities that are required to achieve your goals—and they are in alignment with your values—but you don't want to do them, the next step is to choose if you can delegate them to someone else to accomplish on your behalf.

Feeling Guilty

Scheduling for success sounds simple, and yet when I share with my clients how I schedule my days, they often tell me they do not feel they could do the same because they would feel too guilty putting themselves first on their list.

That is until I ask them if they feel their goals are important to achieve. They always answer that question with a resounding yes.

If you feel the same, then here's the good news: the only way to say no to others without feeling guilty is to schedule each of your days by putting on the calendar the activities that are most important to you to accomplish and will keep you energized from day to day.

When others ask you to do something for them that you do not want to do, you can honestly say that you are already busy—because you are. You are doing what is most important and satisfying to you so you can be of service in the way you feel called to be.

CHAPTER 15

Avoiding Comparison
with Others

Comparison is the death of joy.
—Mark Twain

MOST PEOPLE COMPARE THEMSELVES TO OTHERS on a daily basis. Especially in these days of social media, comparison can be all-consuming.

- "Why did that person's post get more reactions and comments than mine?"
- "Why did that person get the sale instead of me?"
- "Why is that person always so happy and every day is a struggle for me?"

Comparisons Occupy 10 Percent of Our Thoughts

As much as 10 percent of our thoughts involve comparisons of some kind. According to an article in *Psychology Today*, "Research has shown that people who regularly compare themselves to others may find motivation to improve, but may also experience feelings of deep dissatisfaction, guilt, or remorse, and engage in destructive behaviors like lying or disordered eating."[1]

Comparing ourselves to others sure doesn't seem conducive to achieving sales, satisfaction, and success. The *choice* to start being self-accountable to stop comparing yourself to others is required if you want to stay in alignment with your core values, passion, and purpose and make sales faster and easier.

Consistency, Not Comparison

In the new ABCs of selling, the C stands for "consistency," not for "comparison." One keeps you moving forward and the other will stop you in your tracks.

All throughout my day, I avoid comparisons with other people by remembering that what I see on the surface in their present does not tell me what has happened in their past—the trials and tribulations they have experienced, the amount of training they have received, the entirety of their world.

Everyone goes through stages of growth over and over throughout his or her life, just like a rosebush that starts from a seed placed deep in the rich dark soil that eventually blooms many times through its lifetime.

When in the seeding stage, a rosebush has no guarantee that beautiful roses will bloom from it one day. Because I can't keep digging into the area where I planted the seed, I must trust I will eventually see a shoot popping up above ground. During the seeding stage, my job is to keep watering, feeding, and nurturing the soil in which the seed of my goal is planted. I also consult with people who have a green thumb, who may be able to give me "gardening tips."

Grow Your Own Goals

Right now, you may feel you are in the seeding stage of learning the Alignment Marketing Formula because it is a new "seed" that you would like to see help your business grow and develop. Think of this book as your gardening guide. You can think of your sprouts as the leads and prospects that you attract as a result of planting the seeds of the Alignment Marketing Formula.

And in keeping with the metaphor, the blooms are the sales you harvest as you consistently nurture your prospects through the Know, Like, and Trust Principle. At times, just like a rosebush, you will have a resting and rejuvenation stage before the sprouting and blooming stages return.

Now, back to comparisons.

When I tap into the metaphor of seeding, sprouting, blooming, and resting, it's virtually impossible for me to compare myself to anyone else. I do not know how long ago others planted their first seeds. I do not know how much they have invested in time, money, and energy for gardening tips. I do not know how many cycles of sprouting, blooming, and resting they have experienced so far.

Ask for Gardening Tips

As I go through my day's activities and encounter people who appear to be more successful in selling than I feel I am, I can choose to contact them to arrange a time to ask them questions and receive their gardening tips.

When I schedule conversations with these successful "gardeners," I ask the following:

- What goal had you set that produced the results I see you are having? (I may not want to set the same goal as they have. It might not be in alignment with my core values.)

- Who is your ideal audience? (If their ideal audience is not the same as mine, I might not get the same results they have even if I do everything they do.)
- What activities do you do consistently to produce the sales you attract? (Those activities might not be within the circumference of my comfort zone.)

Stay in Alignment with Your Core Values

Elisa Mardegan says she practices daily not comparing herself to others:

> I can remember back to high school when I looked at others and felt I was not as pretty or not as good at sports. When I was in grade nine, I would compare myself to girls in grade thirteen. When I turned thirty years old, I finally realized that no one else is like me and it would be a boring world if everyone was the same. This is also when I realized that people who appear successful now did not just instantly become successful. I remind myself that I do not know how long it took them to become successful.
>
> Tapping into my core values—freedom, courage and family— also helps me to remember to stay focused on my goals rather than making comparisons with others. And I often tell my daughter to stay true to herself and her values, which will keep her from letting others change who she is.

Thierry Alexandre, holding a similar perspective, explains, "I build my livelihood around my own value and self-worth. I know each of us is on a journey. I remind myself I do not know other people's story. I don't know what they are doing behind the scenes. If I do start to compare myself, I know it is time for me to turn my attention back to me and into self-reflection of how I can be and do better for myself."

If you feel you can't resist making comparisons, throughout your day stay focused on comparing where you are today with where you were in the past.

CHAPTER 16

Making Sure Setbacks Don't Break You

Champions keep playing until they get it right.
—Billie Jean King

EACH DAY, WE MAY FEEL as if we are making progress toward our goals. At times we may feel like we are standing still; at other times we may feel like we are losing ground or experiencing a setback.

View Setbacks as a Way to Bounce Back

Imagine stretching a rubber band to its boundary without breaking it. Then let go of the band. It likely bounces back to just slightly larger than its original shape before you stretched it. This stretch happens because the band has not been trained sufficiently to hold the much-larger circumference. It naturally bounces back to what is more comfortable.

The same can be said about our own experiences of creating ever-larger sales goals and attempting to achieve them.

Each day we can choose to train ourselves to hold the circumference of a larger and more successful business. Consistently choosing to accomplish activities toward my goals—scheduling for success—gives me more training, support, and confidence to enlarge my business.

I have also eliminated the word *failure* from my vocabulary, and I ask my clients to do the same. An article in *Psychology Today* states, "Everyone hates to fail, but for some people, failing presents such a significant psychological threat their motivation to *avoid failure* exceeds their motivation to *succeed*. This fear of failure causes them to unconsciously sabotage their chances of success."[1]

Play, Explore, Discover

The vast majority of my clients tell me when we first begin to create a sales and marketing strategy that they feel afraid to fail. I respond with this question: "How could having more information ever be considered a failure?" That instantly snaps them out of focusing on failure.

I then explain that I approach growing my business as a series of experiments. I always *play, explore, and discover* every time I choose to accomplish an activity or goal. That is why I included Billie Jean King's quote at the start of this chapter.

Educational toys for children are designed to provide entertainment while they play, make discoveries, and experiment with new concepts and perspectives. Thierry Alexandre is inspired to play, explore, and discover when he remembers the line from *Mary Poppins* that everything can be made more fun with "a spoonful of sugar."

If we all played with growing our businesses this same way instead of making every activity or decision feel so serious and dire, we would all make more sales and grow our income much faster.

I make sure to remember to play, explore, and discover with every aspect of my business each day. This includes writing my blog, learning how to use a new social media platform, inviting a prospect to have a conversation with me to get to know each other, and so on.

Every Activity Is an Experiment

No matter how much I want to believe that I already know what to do and how to do it, I leave enough room in my mind to allow for new information that allows me to grow my business in the future.

In fact, every suggestion I've made to you so far in this book could be considered an experiment too. Have you been playing with, exploring, and discovering what happens with each one? It's not too late. I invite you to play with each suggestion I made in every chapter and put it into practice as if you are conducting an experiment to see how far your circumference can stretch without bending yourself out of shape or breaking.

The Completion Celebration Experience

I offer to you this process for discovering the results you get each time you play with a new suggestion—whether or not you have achieved your intended result for that activity. I call this process my Completion Celebration Experience.

To do this, I ask myself four questions to prove to myself that whatever the outcome is, my actions were successful in some way. No matter how small (e.g., writing a Facebook post to attract engagement) or large (e.g., hosting a webinar to attract immediate sales from a group of people matching my ideal audience), I ask myself these questions to feel good about what I accomplished and discovered:

1. What were your life and business like just before you started?
2. What result did you want to receive by accomplishing this activity?

3. By doing your best to accomplish the activity, what did you discover you did not know before?
4. What are your life and business like now that you have completed this activity?

I do not ask myself if I achieved the intended result or goal or not. That type of success is not as important as what I discovered along the way. I have always discovered something that I would not know now if I had not attempted to achieve that result or goal.

I agree with author and consultant Norbert Orlewicz, who cautions, "Don't make the setback worse than it is. Stop overanalyzing, take the lesson from it, and move on."

Stephanie Oden approaches expansion this way: "I have a strong belief that I am resilient, and I rely on that belief. If I did not achieve what I wanted to achieve, I give myself permission to have a small pity party and accept that setbacks happen. I also know that next time I will be better prepared to achieve the goal and the process will likely go more smoothly and successfully."

Give yourself credit daily because you stretched a bit further. Even if you bounced back to what has been comfortable in your past, you can return to that smaller width with more knowledge about what to do and how to do it to make the expansion permanent in the future.

Allow that knowledge to keep you inspired to continue taking consistent action, and you will soon attract even more sales, satisfaction, and success daily—just like Jim Packard does: "I am consciously learning to move my focus to the daily practice and not the results."

CHAPTER 17

Self-Acknowledgment and Celebration

Not only does celebrating success feel good in the moment,
but it also sets you up for future success.
—Jodi Clarke

As you complete this journey with me, let's end with a celebration that you accomplished reading this book.

In fact, let's end each and every day with a celebration of all the activities we accomplished throughout the day. Let's celebrate ourselves from morning to night every day.

Celebrate to Stay Consistent

Does celebrating yourself make you uncomfortable? Is it outside your comfort zone to acknowledge yourself for taking action? Is celebrating yourself not on your list of core values? You are not alone, but you are also doing yourself a disservice.

Much research has been done and confirms that celebrating our small and large achievements creates more motivation to continue taking consistent action leading to sales, satisfaction, and success, which is why applauding yourself is a key element in the Alignment Marketing Formula.

While this book is all about staying in your comfort zone, when I suggest to my clients that self-acknowledgment is essential for success, they often tell me they do not feel comfortable celebrating or validating their actions.

If you feel the same, then consider this too: is one of your core values to be of service to others to make sales? If the answer is yes, then I invite you to play, explore, and discover how self-acknowledgment could also be one of your core values.

Do you believe in the Golden Rule to do to others as we would have them do to us? If so, then this rule invites us to celebrate ourselves equally as we would celebrate someone else.

And cheering ourselves on does the body good too. "When you celebrate, endorphins are released inside your body and you feel incredible. When you accomplish something and don't take the time to celebrate, you are robbing yourself of an important feeling that reinforces your success. It reinforces the behavior you want to show up when you face a new challenge or opportunity," according to Bill Carmody, CMO and head of coaching for Positive Intelligence.[1]

Replace Rewards with Celebrations

George Campbell and Jim Packard, in their global best-seller *The Consistency Chain for Network Marketing* write, "Replace rewards with celebrations. People desperately want recognition and appreciation. Let's give that gift to ourselves. Take a moment. Enjoy the accomplishment. Really feel the victory. It's great when other people express their respect for us. It's even better when we earn it from ourselves."[2]

Below are a few of my favorite ways I acknowledge and celebrate me every day to believe in myself and stay motivated to take consistent action toward my goals. Each of these methods of self-acknowledgment also reinforces my sense of self-worth and my belief in myself, which is an essential element in the Alignment Marketing Formula:

Alignment + Belief × Consistency = Sales, Satisfaction, and Success

Let's Go APE

One self-acknowledgment and celebration habit I have created is called Going APE. APE stands for Appreciation Perspective Experience, and I have been Going APE for many years multiple times a day. I am often asked how I am able to accomplish so much each day, and I believe that Going APE is the primary reason.

I Go APE after every activity I accomplish throughout the day. I even Go APE about waking up!

I say privately to myself, "Stacey, I acknowledge and appreciate you for getting out of bed and starting your day."

I continue throughout my day with statements such as the following:

"Stacey, I acknowledge and appreciate you for sending out ten friend requests to people who match your ideal audience."

"Stacey, I acknowledge and appreciate you for having a conversation with a prospect and finding out you are not in alignment so you can move on and make a connection with someone else."

"Stacey, I acknowledge and appreciate you for closing a sale in a satisfying way for both you and your new client."

By Going APE, I hear appreciation all day long, and I no longer rely on others to validate me and my actions. As Louise L. Hay writes,

"You have been criticizing yourself for years, and it hasn't worked. Try approving of yourself and see what happens."[3] When I follow that advice, I feel loved, noticed, and satisfied.

Koriani Baptist feels the same. We both turn to chocolate for small and large celebrations. She says,

> I tell my kids to celebrate themselves, and I encourage my team to do the same. Everything we do for ourselves and others is to be celebrated. This is especially true for Black women. We hardly ever get acknowledged, so celebrating ourselves is *huge*. It is also important to remember that the results (goals, sales, etc.) are not what is important to celebrate. What is important is to acknowledge when we did our best, when we keep our word to ourselves, and when we stay in our comfort zone. By practicing daily the Alignment Marketing Formula and self-acknowledgment, I am ten out of ten on the scale of sales, satisfaction, and success!

Confidence in My Choices

In the past, whenever it came time to make a choice, I would ask someone else to tell me what to do. Putting the power of deciding onto another was my fearful, lazy, wimpy way out of making a decision because I did not trust myself to choose the correct option.

Of course, my internal knowledge and awareness of my core values would always tell me what the right decision was for me. Yet I often did not have the courage to make and act upon it, so I would continuously ask others around me what they thought I should do. Most of the decisions I made in the past were made by other people for me. Because my life was created by other people, I was not in alignment with myself, I was not happy, and I was not achieving the goals I wanted to achieve.

I believe this is what Tony Robbins meant when he said, "It is in your moments of decision that your destiny is shaped."[4]

One morning while brushing my teeth, I realized that all our choices are made from one of two motivations—either love of fear. That day I automatically stopped asking other people what I should do, and I began asking myself five questions that always lead me to the most powerful choices. These questions also give me the courage to make decisions and take action on them.

Love is the harmonizing, empowering force of nature, while fear is the exact opposite. Fear generates anger, frustration, confusion, agitation, and disharmony. Both love and fear are contained within every decision we choose to make. Decisions made from love will be quite different than those based on fear.

Take a moment to consider a decision you made recently. Did you base your decision on the principle of love, or was your decision generated from fear?

If all decisions are based on love or fear, then it makes sense that only five questions are needed to know our options and to see which one we should choose.

The Solution Process

I have created a five-question process to identify if a decision is based on fear or love. I call it the Solution Process. These questions make it easy to know quickly whether a choice is in alignment with your core values in any situation.

Each of us can more readily feel positive and prosperity-minded when we feel our decisions are energizing and empowering and support us to take an action from a sense of desire, passion, commitment, or intention. Here are the five questions:

1. Coming from fear, why would I choose not to do what I am considering?
2. Coming from love, why would I choose not to do what I am considering?

3. Coming from fear, why would I choose to do what I am considering?

4. Coming from love, why would I choose to do what I am considering?

5. Of all the answers I gave to the first four questions, which one did I feel as the strongest in my body (not the best, not the worst, just the strongest)?

The answer to the fifth question is my "gut answer," and I can trust that the answer with the strongest reaction is closest in alignment with my core values. This type of gut reaction can produce a flash of clarity or feelings of peace, safety, or happiness.

One of my clients, Tara Rayburn, used the Solution Process to decide whether she should participate in my Alignment Marketing Mastery Program.

She was attracted to my program at one of the busiest times in her life. Here's how she made the decision whether or not to say yes to herself to participate:

Question 1—Coming from fear, why would I not say yes to the Alignment Marketing Mastery Program?
Answer—I am afraid of becoming overwhelmed with to-dos, which stresses out me and my family. I could appear as a flake for agreeing and then not being able to catch up and keep up and contribute to the deadlines.

Question 2—Coming from love, why would I not say yes to the Alignment Marketing Mastery Program?
Answer—I love my family and know I am no good to anyone or anything when I am in a state of overwhelm. If I cannot contribute with full attention and respect, then it would be more respectful to say no at this time.

Question 3—Coming from fear, why would I say yes to the Alignment Marketing Mastery Program?

Answer—Accepting from fear, I would be missing not only a wonderful opportunity God has put right into my lap but also an opportunity that provides exactly the tools I've needed to achieve my goals. I've been missing the answer to "How do I . . . ?"

Question 4—Coming from love, why would I say yes to the Alignment Marketing Mastery Program?

Answer—I am learning to trust God's hand in my life; I am learning to feel His love and guidance in my gut. I am learning to see the incredible clues and opportunities unfold in front of my eyes. That is what happened here. These words appeared in my mind: "Why not?" and "Love." I felt contrary to my logical sense that by accepting this invitation I would receive and give blessings important to achieving my goals.

Question 5—Which answer felt strongest in my body?

Answer—The answer to number 4.

Tara's decision—I will participate in the Alignment Marketing Mastery Program because taking part will help me on both my career and personal levels, as well as give me an opportunity to offer the blessing of sharing my experiences. It's a win-win!

This decision-making process works that quickly and easily. You can hear the power of Tara's choice coming through loud and clear.

I am often asked if love is always the right answer. Believe it or not, love isn't always the right answer. Sometimes I receive more powerful feelings when I am looking at my fears about doing or not doing something. What I have come to learn is that acknowledging the powerful feelings of fear can be a loving way of taking care of myself. If fear is the most powerful feeling, I trust it. If love is the most powerful feeling, I trust that too.

Time-Outs to Avoid Burnout

We are not machines, we are human beings. We require time to unwind and rejuvenate. One way to celebrate is simply to step away for short periods of time throughout our day. Just like when we were kids, short time-outs contribute to greater creativity, increased productivity, a sense of well-being, a reduction in stress levels, uplifted mood, and stronger relationships.

Let's shift from thinking of time-outs as punishment to viewing them through the perspective of a glorious opportunity—a proactive pause in the activity to catch our breath and to ensure we have a balance between action and nonaction.

When you are feeling that you have been go, go, go and not giving yourself enough time to rest, rest, rest, your mind will start shutting down and resisting doing any more activities. This is especially dangerous if you are still in the seeding or sprouting stage of your goal. When your goal requires a lot of attention, short time-outs are especially required so you don't burn out before you reach the blooming stage.

Carolina M. Billings creates her goals with rewards built in. It looks like this: accomplish a goal, then get a reward, rinse, repeat. Some rewards are small, some are big.

She describes it this way: "I am Latin and was born to celebrate. . . . Even my pity parties are catered. I take a holiday when I achieve a goal, and I create experiences when I travel. One celebration I plan to do with a friend when we attain our goal is we will go to Tiffany's in New York and make a purchase at the 'mothership.' It will not be the same as buying it online. The memories we make will live for years after the actual trip. I like making ordinary things extraordinary."

Carolina understands burnout makes us brittle, and a brittle rubber band breaks much more easily than one that is fresh and flexible.

For an example of why taking these rejuvenation stops is essential, listen to your favorite song and notice the rhythm, melody, and phrasing of how the song is composed. Notice each beat and instrument. Then, notice when each instrument rests.

These rest periods actually create the mood of the music. Without the rests, all there would be is beat after beat. Without the silence, there is no music; there's only noise.

Allow your way of doing business to be a beautiful composition. Throughout your day take a time-out to have fun, do something completely unrelated to the goal at hand, or just quietly reflect on your day and what your future looks like when you have achieved the ultimate level of sales, satisfaction, and success from your comfort zone!

Making the Formula Work for You

AFTER YOU HAVE TAKEN A MOMENT TO CELEBRATE your completion of reading this book, you may be asking these questions:

- What do I do now?
- Where do I start?
- How do I start?
- What is most important to do first?
- Is that all there is to do?
- Can it really be this easy?
- Am I doing it right?
- Can you give me more examples?
- Are you taking on any new clients?

The best way to move forward is to proceed step by step in learning how to master the Alignment Marketing Formula:

Alignment + Belief × Consistency = Sales, Satisfaction, and Success

By taking these steps forward, you will be self-assured that you are in alignment with yourself, your brand, your audience, and your message.

Thierry Alexandre explains it best in one of his social media posts:

Have you ever been told to get outside your comfort zone?
If we think about it for a SEC . . .
Do you like going outside your comfort zone!?
Do you feel at ease or stressed outside your comfort zone!?
Does your mind try to take you out of it or keep you in it!?
So, why are we making ourselves suffer for a concept that has been put on us, and which is making us powerless.
Let's see another concept instead . . .
Does a butterfly grow inside or outside the chrysalis?
Does a chicken [grow] inside or outside the shell?
Do we, humans, grow inside the womb or outside?
Mother Nature gives us all the clues that every strong creation [is] growing from within their comfort zone.
Growth will require some expansion, for sure.
Yet, how about starting doing what you TRULY and DEEPLY LOVE, which is your comfort zone, then expand on it.
Stop doing things that others tell you to do, and that aren't really in a place of LOVE within you.
You CHOOSE what is right for you.[1]

The Recipe to Make the Formula Work for You

You may have noticed as you read this book that each element of the formula requires activation. To activate each element, you need to take simple steps to produce the intended outcome, just as you would with any good formula, or chocolate cake recipe, for that matter.

Here are all eleven steps in order:

Activating Alignment

Step 1—Make your list of core values (see chapter 3). This list is the most important treasure you will ever have. It is more valuable than gold because it defines your comfort zone, which is priceless.

Step 2—Once your list of core values is made, then make a second list of all the ways your values are in alignment with the products or services you sell (see chapter 5).

Step 3—Choose if the products or services you sell help people

- Improve their performance in business
- Make them look and feel sexier
- Make them look more attractive
- Make them healthier or more fit
- Make them more prosperous
- Make them more popular
- Improve their quality of life

Step 4—Answer the questions in chapter 5 to help you identify your authentic passion.

Step 5—Discover how to build trust before you can start selling to your audience (see chapter 6).

Step 6—Identify your ideal audience—the people who have the problems you feel confident and passionate about solving (see chapter 7).

Step 7—Learn how to shift from the me-me-me approach of selling to "I care about you, you, you"—the way to demonstrate you care about their problems and become an authority in your audience's world (see chapter 8).

Activating Belief

Step 8—Craft one simple statement that demonstrates you know the problem you can solve, you have a method or process for solving it, and what prospects can expect as the solution to the problem (see chapter 9).

Step 9—Meet like-minded and like-hearted new friends who match the profile of your ideal audience to shorten the length of time required to build trust and make an offer leading to a sale (see chapter 10).

Step 10—Ditch the script and replace it with asking your prospects discovery questions to explore if they have the problems you can solve (see chapter 11).

Activating Consistency

Step 11—Practice daily the Comfort Zone Expanders from part 5. These comfortable mindset and revenue-producing activities help you remain consistently aligned with your core values and motivated to avoid burnout, increase your enthusiasm, and boost your confidence.

Use these Comfort Zone Expanders to discover a deep sense of satisfaction—a powerful energy generator to stay in action and achieve sales and success.

Be self-accountable—Consistently gather your courage by asking yourself, "In what ways do I *choose* to be able to count on myself?"

Schedule for success—Stop trying to eat the elephant all at once; instead, make a list of every activity (or bite) that is required to achieve your goals. Put them in order of priority into your calendar to ensure the most important ones to accomplish receive the most attention.

Stop comparing yourself to others—Start asking for gardening tips from those who appear to be more successful in the ways you want to grow through the seeding, sprouting, blooming, and harvesting stages of success. Focus on comparing only where you are today with where you were in the past.

Bouncing back faster—Throughout each day, be sure to play, explore, and discover every time you choose to accomplish an activity. Doing business is a series of experiments that provides information on how to stay in action to consistently make sales and grow your business.

Celebrate and acknowledge yourself—All day long, celebrate your small and large achievements to empower yourself to continue taking consistent action that leads to sales, satisfaction, and success.

Now you know almost all my Alignment Marketing secrets. I say *almost all* because I can share only so many suggestions, exercises, and tips in one book.

If you would like more examples of how to practice the Alignment Marketing Formula so you can attract more sales, satisfaction, and success faster, I have something I expect you will enjoy as you gently expand the circumference of your comfort zone. It is waiting for you in the resources section of this book.

Selling from Your Comfort Zone
Discussion Guide

I HOPE THAT READING *Selling from Your Comfort Zone* has inspired you to stop trying to get out of your comfort zone and to stay in alignment with your core values and your authentic passion for representing the products or services you sell.

It may have also raised many questions that would be beneficial to explore with others in the sales and marketing industry or your own sales team.

The following discussion prompts are meant to be considered at the individual and group levels.

Individual

1. What are my core values?
2. What do I feel is my calling or purpose? What do I feel authentically passionate about?
3. Are the products or services I sell in alignment with my core values and my passions?
4. Do the products or services I sell help people in any of these ways:
   - To improve their performance in business
   - To make them look and feel sexier
   - To make them look more attractive

- To make them healthier or more fit
- To make them more prosperous
- To make them more popular
- To improve their quality of life

5. Describe the stages of the Know, Like, and Trust Principle that take place before you can start selling.

6. How does the Build, Engage, and Sell Process connect with the Know, Like, and Trust Principle?

7. What is the difference between the me-me-me approach to selling and the "I care about you, you, you" approach?

8. Before writing a post, producing a live video, creating a brochure or website, or having a conversation with a prospect, you must first craft one simple statement that demonstrates you _____, you have a _____ _____, and _____ _____.

9. Where are you likely to find people who match your ideal audience profile?

10. When you ditch the script, what replaces it?

11. What are your five daily Comfort Zone Extenders?

Team

1. What are the core values of each team member? Are there any core values shared by all team members?

2. What does each team member feel is their unique calling or purpose?

3. What does each team member feel authentically passionate about?

4. Does each team member feel what they sell is in alignment with their core values and their authentic passions? Are there any products or services they feel are not in alignment with their core values and authentic passions?

5. Which of the following do your team members feel your company's products or services can help people do:
    - Improve their performance in business
    - Make them look and feel sexier
    - Make them look more attractive
    - Make them healthier or more fit
    - Make them more prosperous
    - Make them more popular
    - Improve their quality of life
6. Ask team members to describe what the Know, Like, and Trust Principle means to them.
7. Ask team members to describe how the Build, Engage, and Sell Process connects with the Know, Like, and Trust Principle.
8. Ask team members to describe the difference between the me-me-me approach to selling and the "I care about you, you, you" approach.
9. Ask team members to craft their own simple statement to communicate they know the problem their audience wants to solve, the method or process for solving it, and what the prospect can expect as the solution to the problem by purchasing the team members' products or services.
10. Ask team members where they feel they are most likely to find people who match their ideal audience profile.
11. Ask team members to explain what types of questions will they now ask their prospects to ensure they are in alignment and they can solve the prospect's problems.
12. Ask team members how they feel about each of the five daily Comfort Zone Extenders.

Notes

Preface

1. "5 Ways You Can Benefit from Sales Training," Canadian Professional Sales Organization, November 20, 2017, https://www.cpsa.com/resources /articles/5-ways-you-can-benefit-from-sales-training; Norman Behar, "Study Reveals the Importance of Sales Training," Sales Readiness Group, accessed November 28, 2021, https://www.salesreadinessgroup.com/blog /study-reveals-the-importance-of-sales-training.

Introduction

1. Mimi An, "Buyers Speak Out: How Sales Needs to Evolve," Hubspot, October 29, 2020, https://blog.hubspot.com/sales/buyers-speak-out-how -sales-needs-to-evolve.

2. "Women in the Workplace: Why Women Make Great Leaders and How to Retain Them," Center for Creative Leadership, December 2, 2019, https://www.ccl.org/articles/leading-effectively-articles/7-reasons-want -women-workplace/.

Chapter 1

1. "What Happens to Your Body during the Fight or Flight Response," Cleveland Clinic, December 9, 2019, https://health.clevelandclinic.org /what-happens-to-your-body-during-the-fight-or-flight-response/.

2. Stephanie Vozza, "5 Reasons to Stay Inside Your Comfort Zone," *Fast Company*, August 7, 2014, https://www.fastcompany.com/3034025/5 -reasons-to-stay-inside-your-comfort-zone.

3. Anne Gold, "Why Self-Esteem Is Important for Mental Health," National Alliance on Mental Illness, July 12, 2016, https://www.nami.org /Blogs/NAMI-Blog/July-2016/Why-Self-Esteem-Is-Important-for-Mental -Health.

4. Elizabeth Kuster, "Expand Your Comfort Zone," WebMD, accessed November 28, 2021, https://www.webmd.com/balance/features/expand -your-comfort-zone.

Chapter 3

1. Gina Yannotta, "How Do Values and Personality Traits Affect Well-Being?," Maclynn, January 9, 2021, https://maclynninternational.us/blog /matchmaker-comment/how-do-values-and-personality-traits-affect -wellbeing/.

2. Mary Gormandy White, "Examples of Core Values: 100 Powerful Principles," Your Dictionary, accessed November 28, 2021, https:// examples.yourdictionary.com/examples-of-core-values.html; Jennifer Gunner, "What's the Difference between Ethics, Morals, and Values," Your Dictionary, accessed November 28, 2021, https://examples.yourdictionary .com/difference-between-ethics-morals-and-values.html.

Chapter 4

1. Mike Brooks, "How to Evaluate Under-Performing Sales Reps," Sales Gravy, accessed November 28, 2021, https://salesgravy.com/how-to -evaluate-under-performing-sales-reps/; Brian Williams, "21 Mind-Blowing Sales Stats," Brevet, accessed November 28, 2021, https://blog .thebrevetgroup.com/21-mind-blowing-sales-stats.

2. Tracey Wik, "Placing the Right Salesperson in the Wrong Sales Role," Selling Power Blog, November 8, 2018, https://blog.sellingpower.com /gg/2018/11/placing-the-right-salesperson-in-the-wrong-sales-role.html.

3. "No Is Short for the Next Opportunity: How Top Sales Professionals Think," Goodreads, accessed November 28, 2021, https://www.goodreads .com/book/show/23374979-no-is-short-for-next-opportunity.

4. Jeffrey Gitomer, "There's no lotion or potion that will make sales faster and easier for you—unless your potion is hard work. #gitomer," Twitter, November 2, 2015, https://twitter.com/gitomer/status/6611817207171 64544.

5. "Bo Bennett Quotes," Brilliant Read, May 9, 2019, https://www .brilliantread.com/43-best-bo-bennett-quotes-and-networth-2019/.

6. Amy Gallo, "Making Sure Your Employees Succeed," *Harvard Business Review*, February 7, 2011, https://hbr.org/2011/02/making-sure-your -employees-suc.

7. "Women in the Workplace: Why Women Make Great Leaders and How to Retain Them," Center for Creative Leadership, December 2, 2019, https://www.ccl.org/articles/leading-effectively-articles/7-reasons-want -women-workplace/.

8. "33 Inspirational W. Clement Stone Quotes," Gracious Quotes, October 20, 2021, https://graciousquotes.com/w-clement-stone/.

9. Josh Stike and Luke Acree, "4 Powerful Emotions That Sell and Close Deals," August 11, 2021, *Stay Paid*, ep. 272, https://remindermedia.com /podcast/ep-272-4-powerful-emotions-that-sell-and-close-deals/.

10. Patricia Fripp, "Frippicisms," accessed November 28, 2021, https://www.fripp.com/about-patricia-fripp/frippicisms/.

11. Anita Campbell, "10 Quotes to Run Your Business By," November 27, 2006, https://smallbiztrends.com/2006/11/ten-quotes-to-run-your -business-by.html.

12. "Harvey McKay Quotes," All Great Quotes, accessed November 28, 2021, https://www.allgreatquotes.com/quote-167461/.

13. Kendra Lee, "How Believing in Your Products Impacts Sales Success," KLA Group, accessed November 28, 2021, https://www.klagroup.com /how-believing-in-your-products-impacts-sales-success/.

Chapter 5

1. Kate Harrison, "7 Reasons Why People Really Buy," *Forbes*, May 2, 2017, https://www.forbes.com/sites/kateharrison/2017/05/02/seven -reasons-why-people-really-buy/.

2. Mike Renahan, "5 Tips to Quickly Establish Credibility with Prospects," Hubspot, August 1, 2017, https://blog.hubspot.com/sales/how-to -quickly-establish-credibility-with-prospects.

3. Jamie Wise, "5 Ways of Speaking Passionately and with a Purpose," ForbesSpeakers, August 14, 2018, https://forbesspeakers.com/5-ways-of -speaking-passionately-and-with-a-purpose/.

4. Harrison, "7 Reasons Why."

5. Jennie Yabroff, "Julie and Julia: Stop Hating Julie Powell, Please," *Newsweek*, August 5, 2009, https://www.newsweek.com/julie-julia-stop -hating-julie-powell-please-78797.

Chapter 6

1. Jeffrey A. Hall, "How Many Hours Does It Take to Make a Friend," *Sage Journals*, March 15, 2018, https://journals.sagepub.com/doi/10.1177 /0265407518761225.

2. Heather Craig, "10 Ways to Build Trust in a Relationship," Positive Psychology, September 13, 2021, https://positivepsychology.com /build-trust/; Shana Lebowitz, "How to Make New Friends (and Keep the Old) as a Young Adult," Greatist, August 3, 2015, https://greatist.com /happiness/how-to-make-keep-friends.

3. "Albert Einstein: Quotes," Goodreads, accessed March 20, 2022, https://www.goodreaders.com/author/quotes/9810.Albert_Einstein ?page=2.

4. Ali O'Reilly, "What Does Brand Loyalty Mean to Customers?," Rare Consulting, August 22, 2016, https://rare.consulting/blog/2016/8/22 /what-does-brand-loyalty-mean-to-customers.

5. Judith Bowman, "The Importance of Being Acknowledged," *Corps! Magazine*, April 21, 2016, https://www.corpmagazine.com/industry /human-resources/the-importance-of-being-acknowledged; Laura Garnett, "The Powerful Impact of Acknowledging Good Work," *Inc.*, March 23, 2015, https://www.inc.com/laura-garnett/acknowledgment -the-new-charisma-at-work.html; "The Power of Acknowledgment (Part 2)," Learning-in-Action, February 23, 2018, https://learninginaction.com /power-acknowledgment-part-2/; Craig Dowden, "Why You Need to Be Seen," *Psychology Today*, September 11, 2014, https://www.psychologytoday .com/us/blog/the-leaders-code/201409/why-you-need-be-seen.

6. American Osteopathic Association, "Survey Finds Nearly Three- Quarters (72%) of Americans Feel Lonely," PR Newswire, October 11,

2016, https://www.prnewswire.com/news-releases/survey-finds-nearly -three-quarters-72-of-americans-feel-lonely-300342742.html.

7. Bowman, 'Importance of Being Acknowledged."

8. Colleen Francis, "What Your Clients Really Want: The Key Is Acknowledgment," Engage Selling, December 2, 2006, https://www .engageselling.com/blog/what-your-clients-really-want-the-key-is -acknowledgement/.

9. Alisa Yu, Julian Zlatev, and Justin Berg, "What's the Best Way to Build Trust at Work?," *Harvard Business Review*, June 18, 2021, https://hbr.org/2021/06/whats-the-best-way-to-build-trust-at-work.

10. Wayne Huang, "Study: Twitter Customer Care Increases Willingness to Pay," Twitter (blog), October 5, 2016, https://blog.twitter.com/en_us /topics/insights/2016/study-twitter-customer-care-increases-willingness -to-pay-across-industries.

11. A. J. Beltis, "What Is First Call Resolution? Everything Customer Support Pros Should Know," HubSpot, June 9, 2021, https://blog.hubspot .com/service/first-call-resolution.

Part 3

1. "Maya Angelou: Quotes," Goodreads, accessed November 28, 2021, https://www.goodreads.com/author/quotes/3503.Maya_Angelou.

2. "Theodore Roosevelt: Quotes," Goodreads, accessed November 28, 2021, https://www.goodreads.com/quotes/118880-no-one-cares-how -much-you-know-until-they-know.

3. Josh Stike and Luke Acree, "4 Powerful Emotions That Sell and Close Deals," August 11, 2021, *Stay Paid*, ep. 272, https://remindermedia.com /podcast/ep-272-4-powerful-emotions-that-sell-and-close-deals/.

Chapter 8

1. David Meerman Scott, "Nobody Cares about Your Products and Services (except You)," David Meerman Scott, August 18, 2008, https://www.davidmeermanscott.com/blog/2008/08/nobody-cares-ab .html.

2. Chuck Blakeman, "Richard Branson Is Right: Time Is the New Money," *Inc*, September 30, 2014, https://www.inc.com/chuck-blakeman/richard -branson-is-right-time-is-the-new-money.html.

3. Scott, "Nobody Cares."

4. "Cold Calling versus Social Selling: Which One Wins?," Asher, December 10, 2019, https://www.asherstrategies.com/blog/cold-calling -versus-social-selling-one-wins/.

5. Frank Rumbauskas, "Social Media Sales Prospecting Beats Cold Calling, according to Forbes," Business 2 Community, January 7, 2017, https://www.business2community.com/social-selling/social-media-sales -prospecting-beats-cold-calling-according-forbes-01750897.

Chapter 9

1. Brené Brown, *Daring Greatly: How the Courage to Be Vulnerable Transforms the Way We Live, Love, Parent, and Lead* (New York: Penguin, 2012), 12.

2. Makeda Pennycooke, "3 Reasons Why Vulnerability Is Hard," Makeda Pennycooke, July 14, 2015, https://makedapennycooke.com/vulnerability -is-hard.

3. Michael Harris, "Neuroscience Proves: We Buy On Emotion and Justify with Logic—But With a Twist," Salesforce, Medium, May 29, 2015, https://medium.com/@salesforce/neuroscience-proves-we-buy-on -emotion-and-justify-with-logic-but-with-a-twist-4ff965cdeed8.

4. Rockson Samuel, "Why Nobody Cares about Your Business?," Dental Reach, April 5, 2021, https://dentalreach.today/dental-education/why -nobody-cares-about-your-business/.

Part 4

1. Stephen M. Lowisz, "Ditch the Sales Script and Do This Instead," *Entrepreneur*, November 16, 2018, https://www.entrepreneur.com /article/322939.

Chapter 11

1. Ian Altman, "The One Mistake That Kills Sales Scripts," *Inc.*, January 3, 2017, https://www.inc.com/ian-altman/kickoff-2017-with-sales-scripts -that-work.html.

2. Tom Popomaronis, "How to Build a Brand Story That Buyers Emotionally Connect With," *Entrepreneur*, June 8, 2020, https://www .entrepreneur.com/article/351408.

3. Matthew Luhn, "How to Put More Emotion into Storytelling," AdAge, June 16, 2016, https://adage.com/article/digitalnext/put-emotion -storytelling/304463.

Chapter 12

1. Nick Kane, "Beware the Dangers of Rushing the Sales Process," Janek, September 7, 2016, https://www.janek.com/blog/beware-the-dangers -of-rushing-the-sales-process/.

Chapter 14

1. George Campbell and Jim Packard, *The Consistency Chain for Network Marketing* (Success in 100 Pages, 2019), 59.

Chapter 15

1. "Social Comparison Theory," *Psychology Today*, accessed November 28, 2021, https://www.psychologytoday.com/us/basics/social-comparison -theory.

Chapter 16

1. Guy Winch, "10 Signs You Might Have Fear of Failure," *Psychology Today*, June 18, 2013, https://www.psychologytoday.com/us/blog/the -squeaky-wheel/201306/10-signs-you-might-have-fear-failure.

Chapter 17

1. Bill Carmody, "3 Reasons Celebrating Your Many Accomplishments Is Critical to Your Success," *Inc.*, August 12, 2015, https://www.inc.com /bill-carmody/3-reasons-celebrating-your-many-accomplishments-is -critical-to-your-success.html.

2. George Campbell and Jim Packard, *The Consistency Chain for Network Marketing* (Success in 100 Pages, 2019).

3. Louise L. Hay, *You Can Heal Your Life* (Carlsbad, CA: Hay House, 2004), 9.

4. Tony Robbins, "It is in your moments of decision that your destiny is shaped," Twitter, October 17, 2018, https://twitter.com/tonyrobbins /status/1052643381673750528.

Conclusion

1. Thierry V. Alexandre, "Have you ever been told to get outside your comfort zone?," Facebook, September 26, 2021, https://www.facebook .com/thierryvalexandre9/posts/10223469400016317.

Resources

This book can't cover everything when it comes to selling, so here are more resources that will help you and your team get the yeses!

Go for Yes Challenge Five Video Series

Do you feel you would enjoy having support as you practice using the Alignment Marketing Formula so you can attract more sales, satisfaction, and success faster? Great! The free Go for Yes Challenge Five Video Series can be your next step to gently expand the circumference of your comfort zone.

Do you now know why you have been struggling to make sales?

Are you tired of hearing no over and over?

Does it hurt your heart to treat people like targets and numbers?

Would you love to know where to meet people who are ready to buy what you are selling?

Are you ready to makes sales through heart-centered positivity and authentic relationship building?

By now you know I love helping salespeople who are frustrated they are not selling or making a positive difference fast enough.

I have helped thousands of my clients attract their ideal audience, increase their income, and leave a legacy that lives on long after they are gone because they all said yes to completing my fun Go for Yes Challenge Five Video Series.

Each video contains tips for practicing my Alignment Marketing Formula, which makes it possible for you to be in alignment with yourself fully, attract your ideal audience easily, solve the problems of your audience quickly, and increase your income.

The result is more sales, satisfaction, and success! Here is what each video covers:

Video 1—Learn how to authentically sell more product in a way that makes you and your prospects feel amazing.

Video 2—Identify your audience's pain points so you can speak to their soul and inspire them to say yes to purchasing your products or services.

Video 3—Discover the source for never-ending content ideas and daily strategy for what to post and when for maximum results.

Video 4—Choose where to establish your social media presence to meet those who match your ideal audience and are ready to buy from you.

Video 5—Learn the secret sauce to track prospect growth and turn new social media friends into customers, clients, and team members.

Ready to watch? Get *free* access to all five videos at https://www.mylessonhub.com/?m=ditchyourgrind or send an email to goforyeswithstaceyhall@gmail.com.

Go for Yes Masterclass Program

Do you want to know if you are practicing the Alignment Marketing Formula correctly? Would you like to be able to ask me questions as you shift from the old way of making sales to this new way of staying within your comfort zone?

If so, be sure to sign up for my Go for Yes Masterclass Program—my in-depth course, which also includes bonus entry into my Go for Yes Masterclass VIP group on Facebook to support you in attracting customers, sales, and sign-ups rejection-free *without* chasing, convincing, or cold-calling!

Before you say yes to the Go for Yes Masterclass, I have a few more questions to ask you.

How many people are not saying yes to you or your sales team because you don't know how to attract an endless flow of prospects via social media who are ready to buy?

How many people are passing up on your company's products because you or your sales team have been using outdated, ineffective, old-school sales tactics that cause them to reject you and your solutions?

Are you or your sales team members tired of spinning your wheels and wasting your time on social media in dead-end conversations, convincing, cold-calling, and chasing strangers who drain your energy and go nowhere?

Do you agree a lack of a simple lead-generation and effective selling framework that's emotionally satisfying to you and your prospects may already be costing you or your team a great amount of sales?

If your answer is yes to any of these questions, then you know the reasons why I created the Go for Yes Masterclass Program. Here's how the Go for Yes Masterclass Program is designed to solve your problems:

- You or your sales team will learn to attract prospects via social media who are ready to say yes to your products and opportunities so you can make more money now!
- You or your sales team will master the Alignment Marketing Formula framework to connect and close the sale in a way that leaves both you and your prospects feeling amazing.
- You or your sales team will master marketing on social media like the top earners so you stop getting rejected and start getting sales and sign-ups.

- You or your sales team will have powerful support in practicing the daily method of consistency to *never run out of prospects who want to join you.*
- You or your sales team will confidently and authentically *step into conversations, solve your prospects' problems, and get paid quickly.*
- You or your sales team will say goodbye to rejection, cold-calling, and spamming because you never need to feel pushy and sleazy again.
- You or your sales team will take your business to the next level of sales, satisfaction, and success!

Is the value of the Go for Yes Masterclass Program in alignment with your core values? Is there value for you or your sales team in being mentored by me, the creator of the Alignment Marketing Formula, to attract more leads, sales, and sign-ups than you ever dreamed possible?

If so, I invite you to stop going for no and *start the Go for Yes Masterclass.* Discover how to get more people to say yes to you at https://www.goforyesmasterclass.com/?m=ditchyourgrind or send an email to goforyeswithstaceyhall@gmail.com.

Acknowledgments

I AM DEEPLY BLESSED to have attracted into my life and be aligned with some of the most brilliant, kind-hearted, and inspiring people on the face of this planet.

Truly everyone I have ever known has contributed in some way to this book. I mention here those who have played a significant role in bringing the messages shared in this book to the world.

Of course, before I begin the list of clients and business associates who have become my dear friends, I offer my gratitude to God for blessing me with my parents, who taught me from a young age the importance of staying aligned with my core values. As I mentioned in the preface, my father also played a significant role by doing his best to follow all the sales "experts" he was told to follow and showing me why "going for the no" only produces more nos and not sales for most people.

My father did eventually find his true calling. He became a teacher and taught a variety of high school classes. I loved to hear him tell me how much he enjoyed his students. He felt teaching was aligned with his core values.

My husband, Bill, also deserves extra consideration and appreciation. Long before we met, he lived his life staying true to his God-given calling. He demonstrates his core values in the way he serves his clients as a Realtor. I know they agree with me.

Special recognition goes out to my pups—Lucy and Francesca (known as Frankie)—for their cuddles and huddles, as well as their companionship on our walks.

And now, in alphabetical order by first name, I say thanks to those who also lead by example of how to make sales, create satisfaction, and achieve great success by staying in alignment with their core values as they grow their business.

Those I personally interviewed for this book:

Carla Archer, marketing consultant to fitness professionals, launchyourfitbiz@gmail.com

Carolina M. Billings, founder of Powerful Women Today, https://powerfulwomentoday.com

Elisa Mardegan, social media marketing consultant, elisa@elisamardegan.com https://www.elisaannmardegan.com

Jackie Sharpe, founder of Empowering Entrepreneurs Institute, www.JackieSharpe.com

Jim Britt, top 50 keynote speaker and top 20 life strategist, 6-time international best-selling author, http://JimBritt.com

Jim Packard, coauthor of *The Consistency Chain for Network Marketing*, https://www.consistencychain.com

Koriani Baptist, Black Christian mama entrepreneur, blessingkeepers@gmail.com, https://koriani.com

Norbert Orlewicz, business and marketing consultant and trainer, cofounder of MyLeadSystemPRO, https://myleadsystempro.com

Rodolfo Rodriguez Jr., CEO, Virtual Event Sales Team, http://virtualeventsalesteam.com/

Russ DeVan, author of the Success by Design Un-Training™ System, https://www.successbydesign.us

Stephanie Oden, life and business success strategist, questions@stephanieoden.com, www.StephanieOden.com

Tara Rayburn, Healthy Habits Community, https://healthyhabitscommunity.com

Thierry Alexandre, CEO, Thierry V. Alexandre, https://thierryvalexandre.com

Walter Aguilar, president and owner at Power vs Force Coaching http://www. powervsforcecoaching.com

Those who have endorsed this book:

Alexandra Watkins, founder of Eat My Words and author of *Hello, My Name Is Awesome*, https://eatmywords.com

Brian Fanale, cofounder of MLSP, online marketing expert, trainer, speaker, copywriting wizard, https://myleadsystempro.com

Carolina M. Billings, founder of Powerful Women Today, https://powerfulwomentoday.com

George Madiou, CEO and founder of *The Network Marketing Magazine*, https://thenetworkmarketingmagazine.com

Ghazala Jabeen, founder of No.1 Marketing Machine, one of the most successful women in business around the world, https://no1marketingmachine.com

Jerry Yerke, networking marketing consultant, cofounder, corporate executive

Jim Britt, world's top 20 success strategist and speaker, international bestselling author,
https://JimBritt.com

Jim Packard, coauthor of *The Consistency Chain for Network Marketing*,
https://www.consistencychain.com

Dr. Joe Vitale, author of *Zero Limits* and *Hypnotic Writing*,
www.VitaleLifeMastery.com

Kim Ward, CEO, Katie's Mission, best-selling author, speaker and coach,
successwithkimward.com

Sam Horn, CEO of the Intrigue Agency,
https://samhorn.com

Those who provided feedback, testimonials, or inspiration as I was preparing to write this book: Amber Sonsalla, Amelia Johnson, Angela and Ray Shim, Ann M. Cook, Anthony Woodam-Ransom, Barbara Cromwell, Barbara Hope Levitt, Barbara Monroe-Wackman, Begona Lopez Marti, Bernice Cruz, Beth Hartstrom, Beverly Samuel, Bill Carmody, Brenda Jean Wilson, Brenda Martino, Brenda M. Wiener, Brenda Stevens, Brook Adams Visser, Candace Oliver, Carla Almgren, Carla Chicoine Archer, Cecilia Runciman, Charlice Arnold, Cheri Grimm, Christina Rowe, Cindy Harris, Colleen Francis, Cornelia Ionescu, Cortlyn Zierler, Dana Christisen, Darlene Williams, David Boyd, David Meerman Scott, Deb D. Willder, Deborah Neary, Dena Soliman, Denise Kato, Don Bilyea, Donna D. Barron, Donna Wedel, Dortha Hise, Effie Y. Sanford, Elaina Malcolm, Elaine Payne, Elisa Michel, Elisa Van Aspert Mardegan, Erin Morando Cappezzara,

Evelyn Flynn, Gail Woolsey, Geli Heimann, George Madiou, Ghazala Jabeen, Greg Knapp, Ibiyeye Tolulope Kawthar, Ingrid Sherman, Jackie Sharpe, Jackie Walker, Jan Horne, Jane LeVault, Janeen Jackson, Jennifer Hill, Jenny Linden, Jerry McLennan, Jerry Yerke, Jessica Langlais Girouard, Jim Packard, Jodi Clarke, Joan Brunzel Marra, Joe Pizzimenti, Dr. Joe Vitale, Joe Vular, Johanne Pelletier, John Hayes, John North, Joni Denis Goodman, Karen Bromberg, Karen Phelan, Karry Livingston Franks, Kathleen Mitchell, Kathy Guttierrez, Kathy Joy, Kelly K. Lloyd, Kendra Lee, Kerry George, Kevin Duguay, Kim Ward, Kim Wende, Koriani Baptist, Kristina Conatser, Laura Whitney Ribbins, Len Mooney, Lil A. Barcaski, Liz Burhans, Lloyd Chambers, Lois Wyant, Loralee Humphreys, Lori Knight, Lucille Kramer, Lynne Anne Gallaway, M. Susan Patterson, Makeda Pennycooke, Marc Santos, Malia Arnold, Maria Diodato, Marilyn Gracey DeMontrond, Marilyn Jenkins, Mark Smith, Marla Koupal, Martha Brown, Mary Tienken, Matt Seitz, Matthew Luhn, Melanie Hitch Dye, Michelle Landry, Michelle Manning Kogler, Monica Wehri, Monica Wanner, Monika Greczek, Monique Christine, Nick Janek, Nicole Neely, Nikki and Graham Cheetham, Otis Brown, Jr., Patricia Fripp, Patty Lach Daigle, Paul Austin, Peter McIntyre, Rachel Rideout, Rayanne and Walter Aguilar, Rebecca Reilly, Rebekah Cole, Rhonda Randall, Rick Gray, Ron Wilder, Russell DeVan, Sanya Hinchcliff, Sam Horn, Sarah Merrick, Shari Levitan, Shirleen Sando, Shirley Godfrey, Sigrid McNab, Sonika Kruger, Sonya Janisse, Stephanie Oden, Stewart Levine, Sunita Pandit, Suzanne Bledsoe, Tammy and Ed House, Tammy Huntley, Tammy Roach, Tara Rayburn, Tarnisha Garvin, Teresa Selby Fink, Terri Landrath, Terry Hoggatt-Allen, Terry St. Amand, Tiffany Valente LaMonica, Tiffani White, Tina Guimar, Toni Fiest, Toni Smith, Toni Taylor, Tony Schmaltz, Tracey Cook, Trish Borgo, Vince Warnock, Wendy Baila DeAngelis, and Xenia Wignan.

Past and current coaches and associates of MyLeadSystemPRO, who provided their support and encouragement as I was writing this book: Anthony Jackson, Antonio Thompson, Bethany Powlson, Bob Clarke, Brian Fanale (cofounder), Channing Porter, Colin Yearwood, Danny Leonidas, Diane Hochman, Erin Birch, James Fanale, Jesse Kirkham, Jimmy Ybarra, Joe Tarin, J. P. Letnick, Kati Stage, Kay Somji, Keysha Bass, Lindsay Sewell, Lisa Torres, Mark Harbert, Matt Seitz, Melanie Ybarra, Nick East, Norbert Orlewicz (cofounder), Rhonda Reiter, Rodolfo Rodriguez, Shawn Johnson, Steven Krivda, Susan Fisher, Teddye Pearcy, Todd Schloner (cofounder), Troy Boyd, and Valerie Walton.

And to Steve Piersanti and all the staff, associates, and fellow authors of Berrett-Koehler Publishers, it is a truly great honor to have two books now published with your guiding hand and expertise. I am in complete alignment with the company's mission of "Connecting People and Ideas to Create a World That Works for All." Berrett-Koehler sees the world as "a place where our actions as individuals, organizations, communities, and countries embody stewardship, sustainability, quality, partnership, inclusion, and other values that support the well-being of us all. Ultimately, this world must come from all of us, working together."

All of us can help the world get there, one day—and one book—at a time, which is why I acknowledge and appreciate each of the readers of this particular book!

Index

About the Author

STACEY HALL is known as the Go for Yes Gal because of her groundbreaking social media marketing training program called Go for Yes, which has helped thousands of business owners and representatives attract more sales, satisfaction, and success using the Alignment Marketing Formula.

Both her previous books, *Attracting Perfect Customers* and *Chi-To-Be!*, are bestsellers. She is also the producer of the Power of Yes anthology series—a bestseller in the United States, United Kingdom, Canada, and Australia.

She has held marketing management positions with Budget Corporation Rental, FedEx, and the University of Houston prior to launching a successful consulting practice that provides sales and marketing training to clients around the globe.

Stacey is also a leader in the direct-sales industry. She is especially proud of a 2021 launch, in which she enrolled eighty-one new team members in less than three weeks. She has received numerous awards and treasures this accolade—one of many she receives daily—"You are one of the most dynamic people I have encountered on the internet."

She loves the freedom that the sales and marketing industry provides so she can work from home and spend more time with her husband and their pups.

You can reach out to her via

Email: goforyeswithstaceyhall@gmail.com
Facebook: facebook.com/staceyhall1/
LinkedIn: linkedin.com/in/staceyhall1/
Instagram: instagram.com/successwithstaceyhall

Berrett–Koehler
BK̄ Publishers

Berrett-Koehler is an independent publisher dedicated to an ambitious mission: *Connecting people and ideas to create a world that works for all.*

Our publications span many formats, including print, digital, audio, and video. We also offer online resources, training, and gatherings. And we will continue expanding our products and services to advance our mission.

We believe that the solutions to the world's problems will come from all of us, working at all levels: in our society, in our organizations, and in our own lives. Our publications and resources offer pathways to creating a more just, equitable, and sustainable society. They help people make their organizations more humane, democratic, diverse, and effective (and we don't think there's any contradiction there). And they guide people in creating positive change in their own lives and aligning their personal practices with their aspirations for a better world.

And we strive to practice what we preach through what we call "The BK Way." At the core of this approach is *stewardship,* a deep sense of responsibility to administer the company for the benefit of all of our stakeholder groups, including authors, customers, employees, investors, service providers, sales partners, and the communities and environment around us. Everything we do is built around stewardship and our other core values of *quality, partnership, inclusion,* and *sustainability.*

This is why Berrett-Koehler is the first book publishing company to be both a B Corporation (a rigorous certification) and a benefit corporation (a for-profit legal status), which together require us to adhere to the highest standards for corporate, social, and environmental performance. And it is why we have instituted many pioneering practices (which you can learn about at www.bkconnection.com), including the Berrett-Koehler Constitution, the Bill of Rights and Responsibilities for BK Authors, and our unique Author Days.

We are grateful to our readers, authors, and other friends who are supporting our mission. We ask you to share with us examples of how BK publications and resources are making a difference in your lives, organizations, and communities at www.bkconnection.com/impact.

Dear reader,

Thank you for picking up this book and welcome to the worldwide BK community! You're joining a special group of people who have come together to create positive change in their lives, organizations, and communities.

What's BK all about?

Our mission is to connect people and ideas to create a world that works for all.

Why? Our communities, organizations, and lives get bogged down by old paradigms of self-interest, exclusion, hierarchy, and privilege. But we believe that can change. That's why we seek the leading experts on these challenges—and share their actionable ideas with you.

A welcome gift

To help you get started, we'd like to offer you a **free copy** of one of our bestselling ebooks:

www.bkconnection.com/welcome

When you claim your **free ebook**, you'll also be subscribed to our blog.

Our freshest insights

Access the best new tools and ideas for leaders at all levels on our blog at ideas.bkconnection.com.

Sincerely,

Your friends at Berrett-Koehler